Sonja Esbensen

Knitted Lace

in white

"Knitted Lace III"

Grateful thanks to my faithful helpers

Asta, Britta and Hennie,

who have assisted with the knitting of the patterns.

Sonja Esbensen
* 1949 – † 2007

Sonja sadly died after several years of serious illness.
Just before her death she completed this book.

If you have any queries regarding the patterns
then please contact Hennie Bille, preferably in
the morning, by telephone: +45 54 90 10 26
or by Email: billehoj@mail.dk

Knitted Lace in white
© Sonja Esbensen and Akacia Publication, Tommerup, Denmark 2008
Photography: P.E. Nikolajsen
Editor and Lay-out: P.E. Nikolajsen

Printers: Øko Tryk, Videbæk, 2008

ISBN: 978-87-7847-108-6

Foreword

Old handwritten patterns for knitted lace have been used as inspiration for this book. For the knitters of this craft, there is nothing more exciting than the discovery of an old folded pattern at the bottom of a drawer – it just has to be knitted! However, if upon closer inspection several lines of the text appear to be lacking, then the problems arise and skills are tested. There is only one solution: trial and error until the pattern is reconstructed to satisfaction.
With the assistance of my helpers it has been possible to reconstruct 29 patterns for tablecloths and table mats. They are not only beautiful to admire but are also useful in our present times.

I wish you great pleasure with your knitting.

Sonja

It was with great sorrow that we had to say goodbye to Sonja, on the brink of publishing this book.
Sonja was such an industrious soul, who transmitted her enthusiasm for lace knitting to others and encouraged them to experiment with this exciting and artistic form of knitting.
It is our hope to continue her work and to keep her spirit alive.

The helpers

Materials

All of the designs in this book are knitted with DMC Cébélia no. 10, 20 and 30.

Ordinary knitting needles have been used both double pointed needles and circular needles. It is better if the double pointed needles are short because it makes it easier to cast on the stitches. For the large designs up to one meter long, circular needles have been used.

The size of the designs can be altered if a thinner or a thicker yarn is used.. Remember to change the size of the knitting needles as well.

It is always a good idea to make a knitting sample before you start.

Reading a pattern

To make it as easy as possible to decipher a pattern they have all been made with symbols. The pattern report is only shown one time. The report is repeated until the end of the round.
At the next pages you will find a description of all of the symbols and an explanation of how to read the patterns.

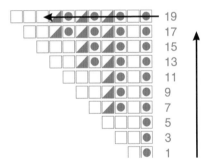

The patterns should be read as they are knitted, from the bottom to the top and from right to left.

In some patterns it has been necessary to describe a single round over more than one line. The same principle applies here: the pattern is read from the bottom to the top and from the right towards the left with just this exception - that the round continues on the line above (see the illustration below).

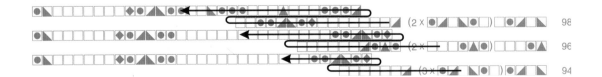

Remember: All rounds not mentioned in the pattern are **knitted plain.**

How to read the pattern

The following symbols are used for describing the patterns:

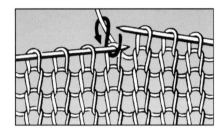

☐ = Knit
A number equals the amount of stitches you have to knit

←☐→ = one round knitted plain.

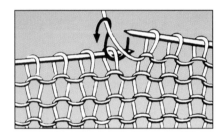

⊟ = Purl
←⊟→ = purl one round

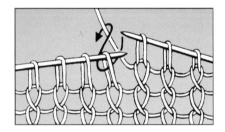

◆ = Knit 1 through back loop

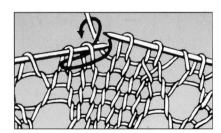

◢ = Knit 2 stitches together
⃞3 ⃞4 ⃞5 ⃞6 = Knit 3, 4, 5 or 6 stitches together

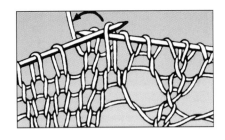 = Slip 1 stitch, knit 1, pass slipped stitch over

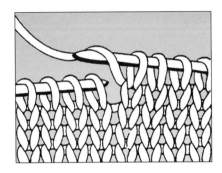 = Yarn over

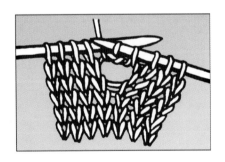 = Yarn over 2, knit 1 and purl 1 into double yarn over on next row, if nothing else is mentioned at the design.

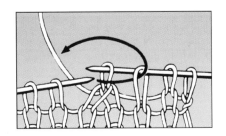 = Slip 1 stitch, knit 2 together, pass slipped stitch over

⊓ = Slip 1 stitch, knit 3 together, pass slipped stitch over

▼ = Slip 2 stitches, knit 2, pass slipped stitches over

◀ = Slip 3 stitches,knit 2, pass slipped stitches over

▶ = Slip 5 stitches, knit 5 together, pass slipped stitches over

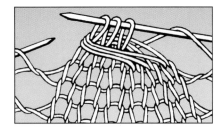

⇆ = Slip 3 stitches, knit 3, pass slipped stiches over

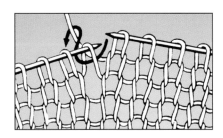

U 2 3 4 5 = Knit 1, 2, 3, 4 or 5 stitches back into running thread between 2 stitches from previuos round

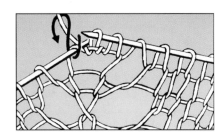

2 3 4 5 6 7 = Knit the number of stitches shown by numeral into the same stitch, alternating, knit, purl, etc.

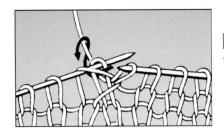 = Cross 2 stitches to the left: knit the 2nd stitch then knit the first stitch, and slip both stitches off the needle.

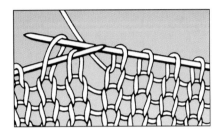 = Cross 2 stitches to the right: knit the 2nd stitch through back loop, then knit the first stitch, and slip both stitches off the needle

M = Stitch

X = Repeat. The numeral shows how many times the sequence has to be repeated.

← M = Slip one stitch from right to left. If there is also a numeral, (ex. ← 3M) slip that number of stitches

→ M = Slip one stitch from left to right. If there is also a numeral (ex. → 3M) slip that number of stitches

* = "Note" See individual patterns for Notes

( ) = Repeat the pattern

How to start

1. The first stitch is formed by making a loop on the yarn and putting it onto the knitting needle.

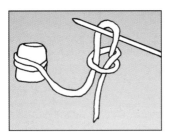

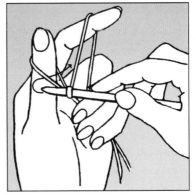

2. Pass the knitting needle under the yarn at the thumb.

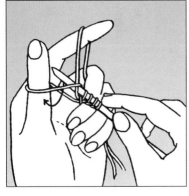

3. Fetch the yarn at the forefinger with the needle. Now the second stitch is on the knitting needle.

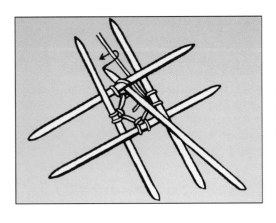

4. The illustration shows how to knit the first stitch in round 2.

5. At the beginning of the work it is a good idea to have a thread in another colour follow up through the work in order to mark the beginning of the round.

How to complete a work

Casting off

Loose cast off. If you knit too tightly it is an advantage to cast off with a knitting needle which is half a number larger than the ones used for the rest of the work. By doing this it can be avoided making the edge too tight.

Crocheting

With models with a crochet edge the procedure is described with numbers. The numbers indicate the amount of stitches which are to be crocheted together and the amount of chain stitches between them. The model at the illustration would be described like this: 3 stitches together with 4 chain stitches between.

Washing instructions

Wash the finished work thoroughly in order to get as much of the filling out of the yarn as posible so that it will accept the starch better.

I use a cornflower starch, which is made like this:

Mix 1 teaspoon starch with cold water. Add boiling water and mix the blend thoroughly. Take care that the blend does not get too thick. Let the mixture cool down until it is tepid. Then rinse the knitting with the starch and squeeze the starch through the knitting a couple of times in order to ensure that the starch is worked into the yarn. At last squeeze the knitting in a clean cloth and now it is ready for getting stretched. REMEMBER to use rustless pins.

Stretching

To ensure that the finished work presents itself as well as possible it has to be washed and pinned out. In most cases it is a great help, or rather a necessity, to make a paper pattern to ensure that the finished work attains the correct shape.

The paper pattern is made on a large piece of paper where the design is drawn in full size and where the finished work is stretched out while it is moist still.

Always draw with a pencil. Ink might rub off especially when the design is moist and it is diffucult to remove again.

Place the moist design on the form and stretch it out with <u>stainless</u> pins. The stretching should be made as diagonally as possible - see the illustrations below.

Paper patterns

The paper patterns may be drawn on cardboard and used again.

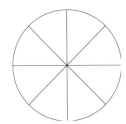

Circular forms.
Draw a circle in the correct size.
You can also divide the circle into halves, quarters and eighths.

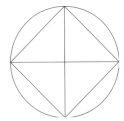

A four-sided form.
Divide the circle into quarters and draw a quadrangle.

A hexagonal form.
Draw the circles as illustrated below. The hexagonal emerges in the centre.

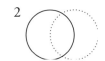

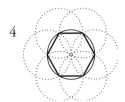
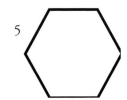

Alice

Knit with DMC Cébélia no. 30
Yarn requirement is about 2 gr
The stretched size is about 12 cm
1 Set double pointed needles 1.5 mm
1 crochet hook 1.25 mm

Crochet edge: Crochet 3-2-3-3-4 stiches together with 7 chain stiches between,
when 3-3 stitches with 1 chain stich between

Chart	Row
◢ ◼ ◣◉◼◣◉◼◉◼◧◢◉◢◉◢◢◉	25
◢ 3 ◣ (3 x ◉◆) ◉◿◉ (3 x ◆◉)	23
7 ◉ 5 ◉	21
7 ◉◉◉	19 *
5 ◉◢	17
4 ◉▲◉	15
4 ◉◆◉	13
4 ◉	11
←☐→	9
←☐→	7
◆◉	5
◆◉	3
←☐→	1

Cast on 8 stitches
All rounds which are not mentioned are knitted plain

Petra

Knit with DMC Cébélia no. 30
Yarn requirement is about 25 gr
The stretched size is about 22 x 22 cm
1 Set double pointed needles 1.5 mm
1 cicular pin 1.5 mm at 40 and 60 cm
1 crochet hook 1.25 mm

Crochet edge: Crochet 2s 1cs - 1s 1cs - 1s 1cs - 2s 1cs - (5 x 10cs 5s 10cs) - 6s with a chain stitch between each, 2s 1 cs - 1s 1cs - 1s 1cs - 2s 1cs - 8cs - 14s with 1 cs between each - 8cs

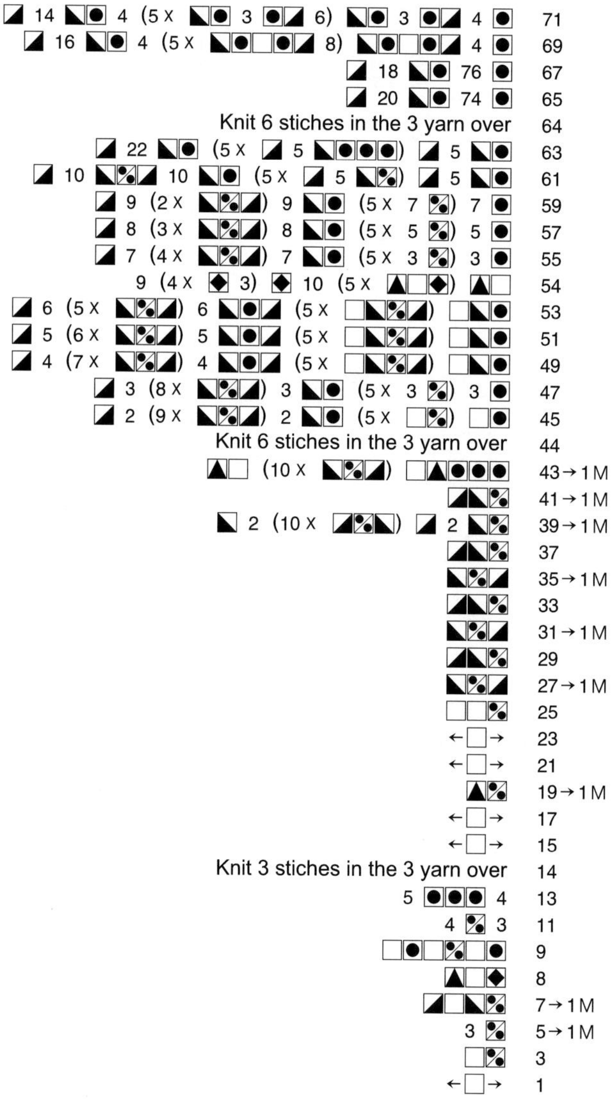

14 �█● 4 (5 x �█● 3 ●◤ 6) �█● 3 ●◤ 4 ●	71
16 ◣● 4 (5 x ◣● ●◤ 8) ◣● ●◤ 4 ●	69
18 ◣● 76 ●	67
20 ◣● 74 ●	65
Knit 6 stiches in the 3 yarn over	64
22 ◣● (5 x ◤ 5 ◣●●●) ◤ 5 ◣●	63
10 ◣▨◤ 10 ◣● (5 x ◤ 5 ◣▨) ◤ 5 ◣●	61
9 (2 x ◣▨◤) 9 ◣● (5 x 7 ▨) 7 ●	59
8 (3 x ◣▨◤) 8 ◣● (5 x 5 ▨) 5 ●	57
7 (4 x ◣▨◤) 7 ◣● (5 x 3 ▨) 3 ●	55
9 (4 x ◆ 3) ◆ 10 (5 x ◤ ◆) ◤	54
6 (5 x ◣▨◤) 6 ◣●◤ (5 x ☐ ◣▨◤) ☐◣●	53
5 (6 x ◣▨◤) 5 ◣●◤ (5 x ☐ ◣▨◤) ☐◣●	51
4 (7 x ◣▨◤) 4 ◣●◤ (5 x ☐ ◣▨◤) ☐◣●	49
3 (8 x ◣▨◤) 3 ◣● (5 x 3 ▨) 3 ●	47
2 (9 x ◣▨◤) 2 ◣● (5 x ☐▨) ☐ ●	45
Knit 6 stiches in the 3 yarn over	44
◤☐ (10 x ◣▨◤) ☐◤▲●●●	43→1M
▲◤▨	41→1M
◣ 2 (10 x ◤▨◣) ◤ 2 ◣▨	39→1M
▲◤▨	37
◣◤▨	35→1M
▲◤▨	33
◣◤▨	31→1M
▲◤▨	29
◣◤▨	27→1M
☐☐▨	25
←☐→	23
←☐→	21
▲◤▨	19→1M
←☐→	17
←☐→	15
Knit 3 stiches in the 3 yarn over	14
5 ●●● 4	13
4 ▨ 3	11
☐☐●☐▨☐●	9
▲◤◆	8
◢◤ ◣▨	7→1M
3 ▨	5→1M
☐▨	3
←☐→	1

Cast on 8 stitches
All rounds which are not mentioned are knitted plain

14

Dagmar

- to be continued

Part A

Crochet edge: Crochet 3-4-5-4-3-4-5-4-3-5 stitches
with 7 chain stitches between

←☐→ 89-92

◣●	87
◣●	85
◣●	83
◆● 9 ●◢ 9 ●	81
◆● 7 ●◢▲▲● 7 ●	79
◆● 5 ● ▲ ●◢● ▲ ● 5 ●	77
◆● 3 ● 2 ▲ 2 ●◢● 2 ▲ 2 ● 3 ●	75
◆● ☐ 3 ▲ 3 ●◢● 3 ▲ 3 ☐ ● ●	73
◆● 9 ●◢● 9 ●	71
◆● 7 ● ☐ ▲ ☐ ● 7 ●	69
◆● 5 (3 x ●▲) ● 5 ●	67
◆● 3 ● ▲ ☐ ▲ ● 3 ●	65
◆● ☐ ● 2 ▲ 2 ●◢● 2 ▲ 2 ● ☐ ●	63
◆● 7 ●	61
◆● 5 ● ▲ ● 5 ●	59
◆● 3 ●▲▲▲● 3 ●	57
◆● ☐ ● ▲ ● ●◢● ▲ ● ☐ ●	55
◆● 5 ●◢● ▲ ● 5 ●	53
◆● 3 ●▲▲▲● 3 ●	51
◆● ☐ ● ▲ ● ●◢● ▲ ☐ ● ●	49
◆● 5 ●◢● ▲ ● 5 ●	47
◆● 3 ●▲▲▲● 3 ●	45
◆● ☐ ● ●◢● ▲ ☐ ● ●	43
◆● 5 ●◢● ▲ ● 5 ●	41
▲● 3 ●▲▲▲● 3 ●◆● 3 ●▲▲▲● 3 ●	39
◢ ◣●☐●●☐● ▲ ●◢●☐● ▲ ●●◆●☐● ▲ ●◢● ●	37
◢ 3 ◣● 5 ● (3 x ◆● 5 ●)	35
◢ 5 ◣● 3 ●◢● 3 ●◆● 3 ●◢● 3 ●	33
◢ 7 ◣●☐● ▲ ●☐● ●◆●☐● ▲ ☐ ● ●	31
◢ 9 ◣● 5 ●◆● 5 ●	29
◢ 11 ◣● 3 ●◆● 3 ●	27
◢ 13 ◣● ●◆● ●	25
◢ 15 ◣●◆●	23
19 ●	21
8 ●◆● 8	19
7 ●◆● 7	17
6 ●◆● 6	15
5 ●◆● 5	13
4 ●◆● 4	11
3 ●◆● 3	9
2 ●◆● 2	7
☐●◆●	5
●●	3
☐●●	1

Knit with DMC Cébélia no. 20
Yarn requirement is about 100 gr
The stretched size is about 82 x 58 cm
1 Set double pointed needles 1.5 mm
1 cicular pin 1.5 mm at 40, 60 and 80 cm
1 crochet hook 1.25 mm

Cast on 8 stitches
All rounds which are not mentioned are knitted plain

Dagmar - *continued*

Part B

169
167
165
163
161
159
157
155
153
151
149
147
145
143
141
139
137
135
133
131
129
127
125
123
121
119
117
115
113
111
109
107
105
103
101
99
97
95
93

Split the work in 4 parts with 96 stitches on each needle
The triangles are knitted on the 2 oppersite needles, purl back.

18

Dagmar - *continued*

Part C

```
                                            ←☐→        234 ← 2M
◆ (2 x ●▲) (3 x ●◣) ●☐● (3 x ◿●) ▲ (3 x ●◣) ☐ (3 x ●◿) (2 x ●▲) ●    233
◆●▲●☐ ▲☐ (2 x ●◣) ● 3 ● (2 x ◿●) ☐▲☐ (2 x ●◣) ● 3 ● (2 x ◿●) ☐▲☐●▲●◆   231
◆●▲●☐ 2 ▲ 2 (2 x ●◣) ●☐● (2 x ◿●) 2 ▲ 2 (2 x●◣) ●☐● (2 x ◿●) 2 ▲ 2 ●▲●◆   229
            ◆●☐● 3 ▲ 3 (2 x ●◣● 3 ●◿● 3 ▲ 3) ●☐●    227
            ◆● 4 ▲ 4 (2 x ●◣● ●◿● 4 ▲ 4) ●◆    225
                ◣● 9 (2 x ▨ 3 ▨ 9) ●    223
            ▲▲● 7 ● (2 x ●▨ 7 ●)    221
        (2 x ◿▲◣) ● 5 (2 x ●●● 5) ●    219
            (2 x ◿ 3 ◣) (3 x ● 3 ●)    217
        ◿ 5 ◣▲◣ 5 ◣ (3 x ●☐●)    215 → 3M
                                ←☐→    213
                        ● 19 ●☐    211
                        ● 17 ●▲    209
                    ● 15 ●◿ ◣    207
                    ● 13 ●◿◿●▲◣●◣    205
                    ● 11 ●◿◿▲ ◣●◣    203
                ● 9 ● (2 x ◿●) ▲ (2 x ●◣)    201
            ● 7 ● (2 x ◿●) ◿▲◣ (2 x ●◣)    199
            ● 5 ● (3 x ◿●) ▲ (3 x ●◣)    197
        ● 3 ● (3 x ◿●) ◿▲◣ (3 x ●◣)    195 ← 1M
        ◆ (4 x ●◣) ●☐● (4 x ◿●)    193
        ◣● (3 x ●◣) ● 3 ● (3 x ◿●)    191
        ◿▲ (3 x ●◣) ●☐● (3 x ◿●)    189
    ◿ 2 ◣ (2 x ●◣) ● 3 ● (2 x ◿●)    187
    ◿ 4 ◣ (2 x ●◣) ●☐● (2 x ◿●)    185
        ◿ 6 ◣●◣● 3 ●◿◿    183
        ◿ 8 ◣●◣● ●◿◿    181
            ◿ 10 ◣● 3 ●    179
            ◿ 12 ◣●☐●    177
                16 ●    175
                ←☐→    173
                ←☐→    171
```

Pick up 80 stiches on each side. Together with 2 x 96 stitches it makes 512 stitches. Knit part C.

Helga

Crochet edge: Crochet 2-3-5-3-5-4-3-4-5-3-5-3 with
7 chain stitches between

* = On the plain round knit 2 stitches in the yarn over
** = On the plain round knit 3 stitches in the 2 yarn over

Knit with DMC Cébélia no. 20
Yarn requirement is about 30 gr
The stretched size is about 39 cm
1 Set double pointed needles 1.5 mm
1 cicular pin 1.5 mm at 40 and 60 cm
1 crochet hook 1.25 mm

Cast on 8 stitches
All rounds which are not mentioned are knitted plain

Sofie

Knit with DMC Cébélia no. 30
Yarn requirement is about 8 gr
The stretched size is about 20 cm
1 Set double pointed needles 1.5 mm
1 crochet hook 1.25 mm

Crochet edge: Crochet 10 x 3 stitches with 7 chain stitces between and 2 x 3 stitches with a chain stitch between.

```
                                          ←□→      40→2M
                        ● 6 (3 x ●◆● 6) ●◤          39
                    (3 x ● 4 ●◆) ● 4 ●◤◣◤           37
                 (3 x ● 2 ●◆) ● 2 ●◤◣◪◤             35
              ● 3 ●◆● 3 ●◤ (2 x ◥◪◤) ◤              33←1M
              ◤● ●◆● ●◤ (3 x ◥◪◤)                   31
              ●◤◣● ●◤ (3 x ◥◪◤) ◥●                  29
                    ◥◪◤● (4 x ◥◪◤)                  27
              ● (2 x 2 ◪) ◤ (2 x ◥◪◤) ◥●            25
                        ● 2 ●◤ 11 ◥                 23
                              ◪ 15                  21
                              ←□→                   19
                              ←□→                   17
                        6 ● ● 6                     15
                        5 ● ● 5                     13
                        4 ● ● 4                     11
                          4 ● 4                      9
                          ←□→                        7
                       (4 x ●□)                      5
                       (2 x ●□)                      3
                          ●□                         1
```

Cast on 8 stitches and knit 1 round plain
All rounds which are not mentioned are knitted plain

Vibeke

Crochet edge: Crochet 4 stitches with 7 chain stitches between

←□→ 100
(25 x) 99
(24 x) 97
(4 x 7 · 7) 7 · 7 · 95
(4 x 6 · 6) 6 · 6 · 93
(4 x 5 · 5) 5 · 5 · 91
(4 x 4 · 4) 4 · 4 · 89
5 · (4 x 10 · ·) 10 · 5 · 87
(4 x 8 · ·) 8 · 85 ←4M
1 · 4 · 3 · 3 · 4 · 83 * *
4 · 83 * *
· 4 (4 x · 4) · 81
(4 x ·) · 79
· 77
(2 x ·) · 77
· (3 x ·· ··) (3 x ·) · (4 x ·) · 75
· (3 x ·· 3 ·· 2 ·) (2 x ·) · 3 (3 x ·) · 73
· (3 x ·· ·· 4 ·) (2 x ·) · (3 x ·) · 71
· (3 x ·· 3 ·· 6 ·) ·· 3 (2 x ·) · 69
5 · (3 x ·· ·· 8 ·) ·· 3 · · 5 67
· 3 · 10 · 3 · 3 · 3 · 3 · 10 · 3 · 65 ←4M
· 4 · 4 · 3 · 63 * *
3 · 4 · 4 · 63 * *
· 6 · 6 · 4 · 4 · 6 · 6 · 61
· 5 · 5 · 5 · 5 · 59
· 4 · 4 · 5 · 2 · 5 · 4 · 4 · 57
· 10 · 5 · 4 · 5 · 10 · 55
· 8 · 5 · 2 · 5 · 8 · 53
· 6 · 5 · 2 · 5 · 6 · 51
· 4 · 5 · 3 · 3 · 5 · 4 · 49
5 · 4 · 4 · 4 · 4 · 5 · 47
3 · 2 · 3 · 5 · 5 · 3 · 2 · 3 · 45 ←1M
2 · 4 · 5 · 2 · 5 · 4 · 2 · 43
· 8 · 5 · 4 · 5 · 8 · 41
6 · 5 · 6 · 5 · 6 · 39
4 · 5 · 8 · 5 · 4 · 37 ←1M
· 5 · 10 · 5 · 35
5 · 4 · 4 · 5 · 33
4 · 6 · 6 · 4 · 31
5 · 5 · 5 · 5 · 29
5 · 4 · 4 · 5 27
5 · 10 · 5 · 25
5 · 8 · 5 23
5 · 6 · 5 21
5 · 4 · 5 19
5 · · 5 17
· 2 · 2 · 2 · 15 ←1M
· 4 · 13 →1M
2 (2 x · 2) 11
· · 9
7 *
←□→ 5
3
←□→ 1

Knit with DMC Cébélia no. 20
Yarn requirement is about 22 gr
The stretched size is about 30 x 30 cm
1 Set double pointed needles 1.5 mm
1 cicular pin 1.5 mm at 40 and 60 cm
1 crochet hook 1.25 mm

* = in round 8 knit 4 stitches in the double yarn over
** = in round 64 and round 84 knit 8 stitches in the 3 yarn over

Cast on 8 stitches
All rounds which are not mentioned are knitted plain

25

Margrethe

Knit with DMC Cébélia no. 30
Yarn requirement is about 13 gr
The stretched size is about 25 cm
1 Set double pointed needles 1.5 mm
1 crochet hook 1.25 mm

Crochet edge: Crochet 3 stitches with 7 chain stitches between

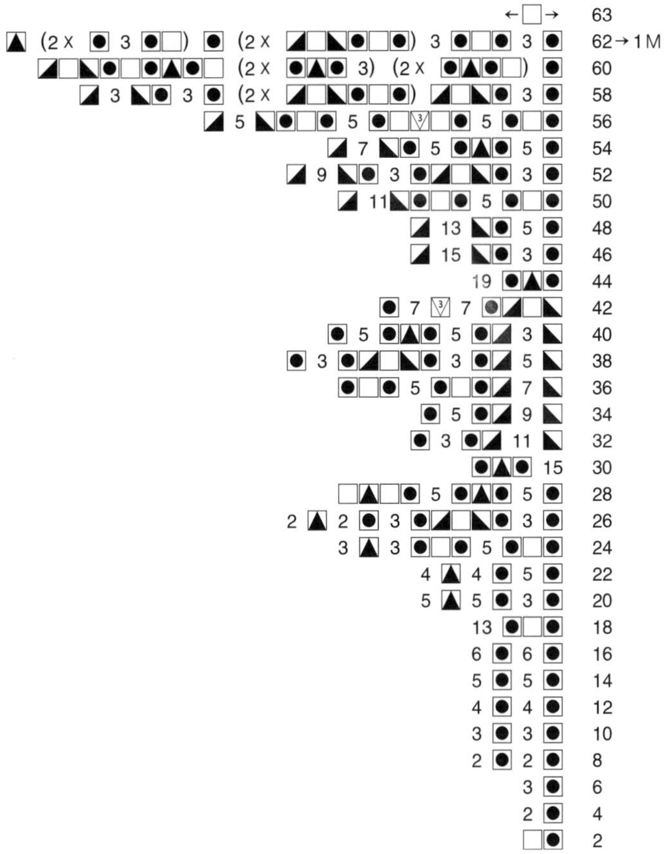

```
                                              ← □ →      63
▲ (2 x ● 3 ● ) ● (2 x ◢ ◣● ● )) 3 ● ● 3 ●    62 → 1 M
  ◢ ◣● ●▲● □ (2 x ●▲● 3) (2 x ●▲● ) ●         60
  ◢ 3 ◣● 3 ● (2 x ◢ ◣● ● ) ◢ ◣● 3 ●           58
    ◢ 5 ◣● ● 5 ● � ● ● 5 ● ● ●               56
        ◢ 7 ◣● 5 ●▲● 5 ●                        54
      ◢ 9 ◣● 3 ●◢ ◣● 3 ●                        52
        ◢ 11◣● ● 5 ● ●                          50
          ◢ 13 ◣● 5 ●                           48
          ◢ 15 ◣● 3 ●                           46
              19 ●▲●                             44
          ● 7 ⊻ 7 ●◢ ◣                          42
        ● 5 ●▲● 5 ●◢ 3 ◣                        40
      ● 3 ●◢ ◣● 3 ●◢ 5 ◣                        38
        ● ● 5 ● ●◢ 7 ◣                          36
          ● 5 ●◢ 9 ◣                            34
        ● 3 ●◢ 11 ◣                             32
          ●▲● 15                                30
        □▲● 5 ●▲● 5 ●                           28
  2 ▲ 2 ● 3 ●◢ ◣● 3 ●                           26
    3 ▲ 3 ● ● 5 ● ●                             24
      4 ▲ 4 ● 5 ●                               22
      5 ▲ 5 ● 3 ●                               20
          13 ● ●                                18
          6 ● 6 ●                               16
          5 ● 5 ●                               14
          4 ● 4 ●                               12
          3 ● 3 ●                               10
          2 ● 2 ●                                8
              3 ●                                6
              2 ●                                4
            □ ●                                  2
```

Cast on 8 stitches and knit 1 round plain
All rounds which are not mentioned are knitted plain

Ditte Marie

Knit with DMC Cébélia no. 30
Yarn requirement is about 5 gr
The stretched size is about 23 cm
1 Set double pointed needles 1.5 mm
1 cicular pin 1.5 mm at 40 cm
1 crochet hook 1.25 mm

Crochet edge: Crochet 3-7-5-7-5-7-5 stitches with 7 chain stitches
between and 7-3-3 stitches with 1 double crochet between

Cast on 8 stitches and knit 1 round plain
All rounds which are not mentioned are knitted plain

Else

Crochet edge: Knit 3 stiches forward and croche 5-3-5-3-5-3-5-3-5-3-5-3-5-3-5-4 stiches with 6 chain stiches between.
Crochet another round: crochet from chain to chain with 7 chain stiches between.

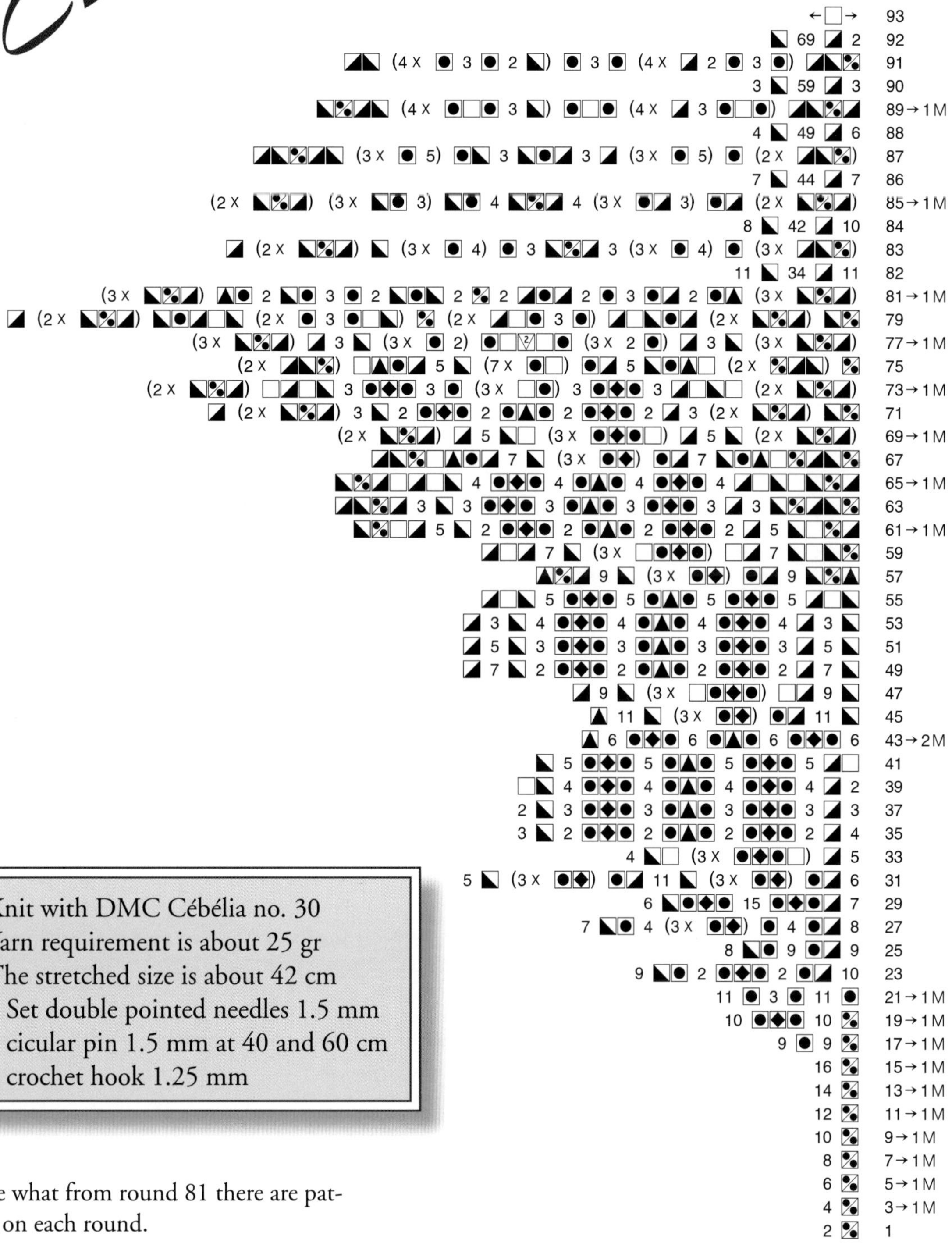

Knit with DMC Cébélia no. 30
Yarn requirement is about 25 gr
The stretched size is about 42 cm
1 Set double pointed needles 1.5 mm
1 cicular pin 1.5 mm at 40 and 60 cm
1 crochet hook 1.25 mm

Note what from round 81 there are pattern on each round.

Cast on 8 stitches and knit 1 round plain
All rounds which are not mentioned are knitted plain

Knit with DMC Cébélia no. 20
Yarn requirement is about 15 gr
The stretched size is about 24 cm
1 Set double pointed needles 1.5 mm
1 cicular pin 1.5 mm at 40 cm
1 crochet hook 1.25 mm

Crochet edge: Crochet 5-6-5 stitches with 7 chain stitches between - 1 chain stitch - 3 stitches - 1 chain stitch 5-6-5 stitches with 7 chain stitches between

Cast on 8 stitches and knit 1 round plain
All rounds which are not mentioned are knitted plain

* = in round 12 and round 28 knit 12 stitches in the 3 yarn over
** = in round 46 knit 15 stitches in the 3 yarn over

Amalie

Knit with DMC Cébélia no. 30
Yarn requirement is about 80 gr
The stretched size is about 76 cm
1 Set double pointed needles 1.5 mm
1 cicular pin 1.5 mm at 40, 60, 80 and 100 cm

Cast off loosly. Maybe with a needle a number larger, in order not to make the edge too tight

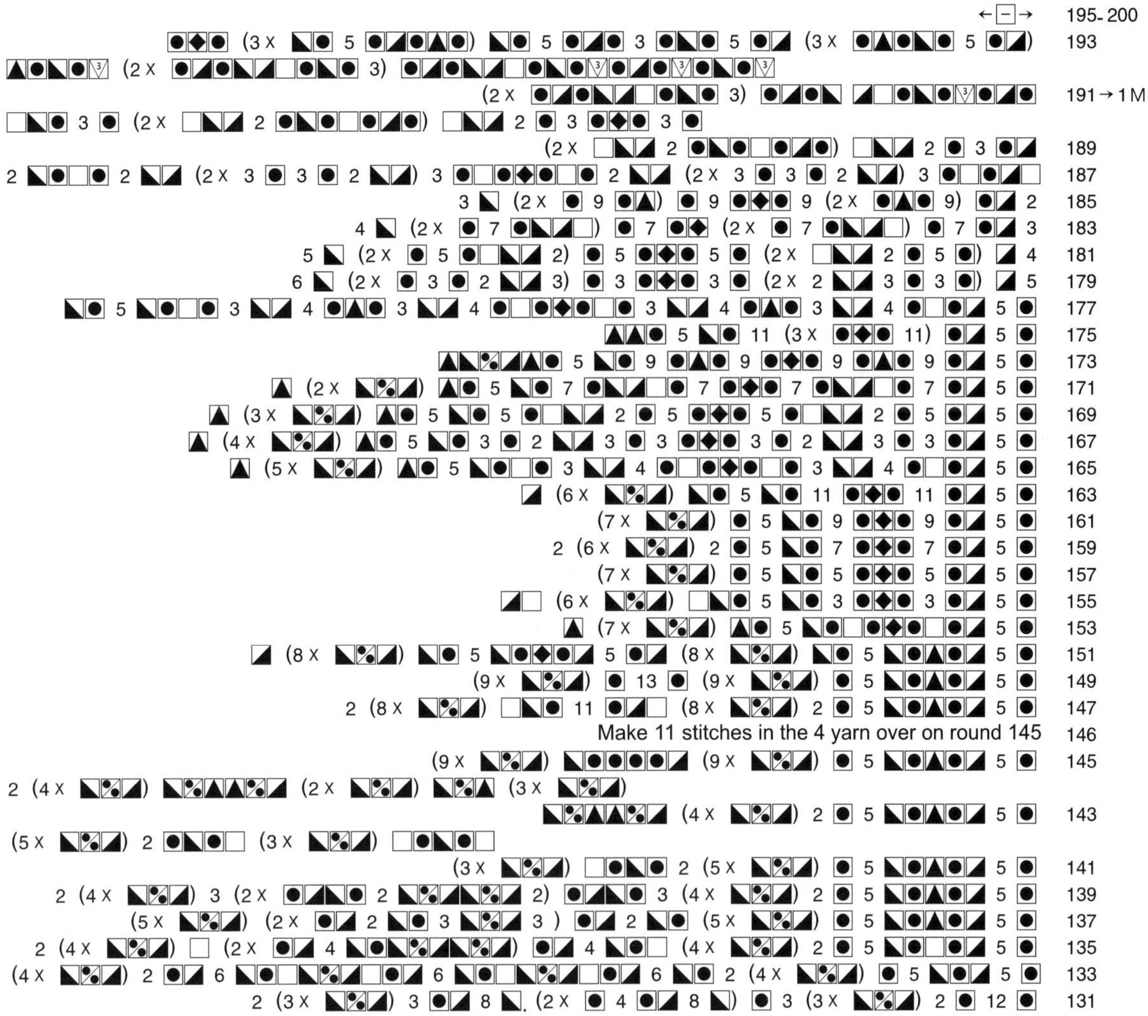

←⎯→   195‑ 200

Chart row	Row number
● ◆ ● (3 x ◣● 5 ●◢◣●◢●) ◣● 5 ●◢◣ 3 ●◣● 5 ●◢ (3 x ●◢◣●◣● 5 ●◢)	193
▲●◣●�Ⅴ (2 x ●◢◣●◣◢ ●◣● 3) ●◢◣●◣ ●◣●◣Ⅴ●◢◣◢Ⅴ●◣●	
(2 x ●◢◣●◣◢ ●◣● 3) ●◢◣● ◢ ●◣●◣Ⅴ●◢◣◢	191 → 1 M
◻◣● 3 ● (2 x ◻◣◢ 2 ●◣● ●◢◣●) ◻◣◢ 2 ● 3 ●◆● 3 ●	
(2 x ◻◣◢ 2 ●◣● ●◢◣●) ◻◣◢ 2 ● 3 ●◢	189
2 ◣●◻ ●◢ 2 ◣◢ (2 x 3 ● 3 ● 2 ◣◢) 3 ● ●◆●◣● 2 ◣◢ (2 x 3 ● 3 ● 2 ◣◢) 3 ● ●◣◢	187
3 ◣ (2 x ● 9 ●▲) ● 9 ●◆● 9 (2 x ●◢▲ 9) ●◢ 2	185
4 ◣ (2 x ● 7 ●◣◢◻) ● 7 ◆● (2 x ● 7 ●◣◢) ● 7 ●◣◢ 3	183
5 ◣ (2 x ● 5 ● ◣◢ 2) ● 5 ●◆● 5 ● (2 x ◻◣◢ 2 ● 5 ●) ◢ 4	181
6 ◣ (2 x ● 3 ● 2 ◣◢ 3) ● 3 ●◆● 3 ● (2 x 2 ◣◢ 3 ● 3 ●) ◢ 5	179
◣● 5 ◣● ●◻ 3 ◣◢ 4 ●◢▲● 3 ◣◢ 4 ● ●◆● ●◻ 3 ◣◢ 4 ●◢▲● 3 ◣◢ 4 ● ●◢ 5 ◢	177
▲▲● 5 ◣● 11 (3 x ●◆● 11) ●◢ 5 ●◢	175
▲◣Ⅴ◢▲◢ 5 ◣● 9 ●◢▲● 9 ●◆● 9 ●◢▲● 9 ●◢ 5 ●◢	173
▲ (2 x ◣Ⅴ◢) ▲● 5 ◣● 7 ●◣◢▲● 7 ●◆● 7 ●◣◢▲● 7 ●◢ 5 ●◢	171
▲ (3 x ◣Ⅴ◢) ▲● 5 ◣● 5 ● ◣◢ 2 ● 5 ●◆● 5 ● ◣◢ 2 ● 5 ●◢ 5 ●◢	169
▲ (4 x ◣Ⅴ◢) ▲● 5 ◣● 3 ● 2 ◣◢ 3 ● 3 ●◆● 3 ● 2 ◣◢ 3 ● 3 ●◢	167
▲ (5 x ◣Ⅴ◢) ▲● 5 ◣● ●◻ 3 ◣◢ 4 ● ●◆● ●◻ 3 ◣◢ 4 ● ●◢ 5 ●◢	165
◢ (6 x ◣Ⅴ◢) ◣● 5 ◣● 11 ●◆● 11 ●◢ 5 ●◢	163
(7 x ◣Ⅴ◢) ● 5 ◣● 9 ●◆● 9 ●◢ 5 ●◢	161
2 (6 x ◣Ⅴ◢) 2 ● 5 ◣● 7 ●◆● 7 ●◢ 5 ●◢	159
(7 x ◣Ⅴ◢) ● 5 ◣● 5 ●◆● 5 ●◢ 5 ●◢	157
◢ ◻ (6 x ◣Ⅴ◢) ◻◣● 5 ◣● 3 ●◆● 3 ●◢ 5 ●◢	155
▲ (7 x ◣Ⅴ◢) ● 5 ◣● ●◆● ●◢ 5 ●◢	153
◢ (8 x ◣Ⅴ◢) ● 5 ◣●◆●◢ 5 ●◢ (8 x ◣Ⅴ◢) ◣● 5 ◣●◢▲●◢ 5 ●◢	151
(9 x ◣Ⅴ◢) ● 13 ● (9 x ◣Ⅴ◢) ● 5 ◣●◢ 5 ●◢	149
2 (8 x ◣Ⅴ◢) ◻● 11 ●◢ ◻ (8 x ◣Ⅴ◢) 2 ● 5 ◣●◢▲●◢ 5 ●◢	147
Make 11 stitches in the 4 yarn over on round 145	146
(9 x ◣Ⅴ◢) ◣●◻◻●◻◢Ⅰ (9 x ◣Ⅴ◢) ● 5 ◣●◢▲●◢ 5 ●◢	145
2 (4 x ◣Ⅴ◢) ◣Ⅴ▲▲◢ (2 x ◣Ⅴ◢) ◣Ⅴ▲ (3 x ◣Ⅴ◢)	
(5 x ◣Ⅴ◢) 2 ●◣● ◻ (3 x ◣Ⅴ◢) ◻●◣●	
◣Ⅴ▲▲◣◢ (4 x ◣Ⅴ◢) 2 ● 5 ◣●◢▲●◢ 5 ●◢	143
(3 x ◣Ⅴ◢) ◻◣●◢ 2 (5 x ◣Ⅴ◢) ● 5 ◣●◢▲●◢ 5 ●◢	141
2 (4 x ◣Ⅴ◢) 3 (2 x ●◢▲●◢ 2 ◣Ⅴ▲◣Ⅴ 2) ●◢▲●◢ 3 (4 x ◣Ⅴ◢) 2 ● 5 ◣●◢▲●◢ 5 ●◢	139
(5 x ◣Ⅴ◢) (2 x ●◢ 2 ◣● 3 ◣Ⅴ◢ 3) ●◢ 2 ◣● (5 x ◣Ⅴ◢) ● 5 ◣●◢ 5 ●◢	137
2 (4 x ◣Ⅴ◢) ◻ (2 x ●◢ 4 ◣●◢◣Ⅴ▲◢ ◣◢) ●◢ 4 ◣● (4 x ◣Ⅴ◢) 2 ● 5 ◣●◢ 5 ●◢	135
(4 x ◣Ⅴ◢) 2 ●◢ 6 ◣● ◻◣Ⅴ◢ ●◢ 6 ◣● ◣Ⅴ◢ ●◢ 6 ◣● 2 (4 x ◣Ⅴ◢) ● 5 ◣●◢ 5 ●◢	133
2 (3 x ◣Ⅴ◢) 3 ●◢ 8 ◣ (2 x ● 4 ●◢ 8 ◣) ● 3 (3 x ◣Ⅴ◢) 2 ● 12 ●	131

- to be continued

35

(4 x ⬛◻◿) ◻◢ 10 ◣● (2 x 2 ◻◢ 10 ◣●) (4 x ⬛◻◿) ● 10 ●   129

2 (2 x ⬛◻◿) ⬛◻◤◥ (3 x ◻◢ 12 ◣●) ◿◣◻◿ (2 x ⬛◻◿) 2 ● 8 ●   127

◤◻◿ (2 x ⬛◻◿) ◣◻ ◻◢◿ 7 ●◆●

13 ●◆● 5 ◣ 6 ●◆● 7 ◿◣ ● ◻ ◿ (2 x ⬛◻◿) ⬛◻◤● 6   125

● ◻ ◿ (2 x ⬛◻◿) ⬛◻◤◣●◻◿ 2 ◣ 6 (2 x ●◆● 11) ●◆● 6 ◿ 2 ◣◻◤◻◿ (2 x ⬛◻◿) ◣ ● 6   123

●◤◻◿ (2 x ⬛◻◿)◣ ◻◿ 4 ◣ 5 (2 x ●◆● 9) ●◆● 5 ◿ 4 ◣◻ ◿ (2 x ⬛◻◿) ⬛◻◤● 6   121

● ◻ ◿ (3 x ⬛◻◿) ◻◢ 6 ◣ 4 (2 x ●◆● 7) ●◆● 4 ◿ 6 ◣● (3 x ⬛◻◿) ◣ ◻ ● 6   119

◤◻◿ (2 x ⬛◻◿) ◻●◢ 5 ⊘ ◣ 3

(2 x ●◆● 5) ●◆● 3 ◿ ◻◨ 5 ◣● ◻ (2 x ⬛◻◿) ⬛◻◤● 6   117

● ◿ ◻ (2 x ⬛◻◿) 2 ●◿ 5 ⊘⊘ ◣ 2 (2 x ●◆● 3)

●◆● 2 ◿ ◨◨ 5 ◣● 2 (2 x ⬛◻◿) ◻ ◣● 6   115

●◤◻◤◥◻◿ 3 ●◿ 5 ⊘⊘⊘ ◣ (3 x ◻●◆●) ◻◿ ◨◨◨ 5 ◣● 3 ⬛◻◤◻◤◥● 6   113

● ◻ ◿ (2 x ⬛◻◿) ● 6 ⊘⊘⊘⊘●◤●◆●◤●◨◨◨◨ 6 ● (2 x ⬛◻◿) ◣ ◻ ● 6   111

●◤◻◤◥◻◿ 2 ● 6 ⊘⊘⊘⊘ ◻ ◿ ◻ ◨◨◨◨ 6 ● 2 ⬛◻◤◻◤◥● 6   109

◻ ● ◿ (2 x ⬛◻◿) ● 6 ⊘⊘⊘⊘◿⊘ ◣◨◨◨◨ 6 ● (2 x ⬛◻◿) ◻ ◻ ● 6   107

●◤◻◤◥◻◿ 2 ● 6 ⊘⊘⊘⊘ ◿⊘◨ ◣ ◨◨◨ 6 ● 2 ⬛◻◤◻◤◥● 6   105

◻ ● ◿ (2 x ⬛◻◿) ● 6 ⊘⊘⊘◿⊘⊘◨◨ ◣◨◨◨ 6 ● (2 x ⬛◻◿) ◻ ◻ ● 6   103

●◤◻◤◥◻◿ 2 ● 6 ⊘⊘⊘ ◿⊘⊘◨◨ ◣◨◨◨ 6 ● 2 ⬛◻◤◻◤◥● 6   101

● ◻ ◿ (2 x ⬛◻◿) ● 8 ⊘⊘◿⊘⊘⊘◨◨ ◿ ◨ 8 ● (2 x ⬛◻◿) ◻ ◻ ● 6   99

●◤◻◤◥◻◿ 2 ● 11◿⊘⊘⊘◨◨ ◿ 11 ● 2 ⬛◻◤◻◤◥● 6   97

● ◻ ◿ (2 x ⬛◻◿) ● 9 ◿◿ ◨ ◣ ◨ ◣● 9 ● (2 x ⬛◻◿) ◣ ◻ ● 6   95

●◤◻◤◥◻◿ 2 ● 7 ◻◿ ◿◨◨◨◨◨ ◿◨ 7 ● 2 ⬛◻◤◻◤◥● 6   93

● ◻ ◿ (2 x ⬛◻◿) ● 5 ◻◿ ◿◨◣ ◿⊘⊘◨◨ ◿◨ ◣● 5 ● (2 x ⬛◻◿) ◣ ◻ ● 6   91

● (2 x ⬛◻◿) 2 ● 3 ●◿ ⊘⊘◿ ◣◿⊘◨◨◨◨ ◿◨◨ ◣● 3 ● 2 (2 x ⬛◻◿) ● 6   89

● ◻ (2 x ⬛◻◿) ● ◻◿ 3 ⊘⊘◿ ◣ ◿⊘◨◨◨◨ ◿◨◨ 3 ◣● ● (2 x ⬛◻◿) ◻ ● 6   87

● 2 ⬛◻◤◿ ◣● 11 ●◣◻● ⊘⊘◿◨◨●◤● 11 ◻◿ ⬛◻◤◿ 2 ● 6   85

● 3 ⬛◻◤◻● 9 ●◤◣● ⊘⊘◨◨●◤● 9 ●◤◣◿ 3 ● 6   83

●◤◻◤◥◻◤◥ (2 x ● 7 ●◿ 2 ◣) ● 7 ●◤◻◤◥◻◤◥● 6   81

● ◻ ◿◻◤◿ 2 ◣ (2 x ● 5 ●◿ 4 ◣) ● 5 ●◿ 2 ⬛◻◤◿ ● 6   79

●◤◻◤◥◻◤◥◻ ◣ (2 x ● 3 ●◿ ⬛◻◿ ◻) ● 3 ◿ ◻◤◻◤◥● 6   77

● ◻ ◿ (2 x ⬛◻◿) ◣● ◻◿ (2 x ⬛◻◿) ◣●◤● ◿ (2 x ⬛◻◿) ◣● ◻◿ (2 x ⬛◻◿) ◣ ◻ ● 6   75

●◤◻◿ (2 x ⬛◻◿) ● (3 x ⬛◻◿) ●◤● (3 x ⬛◻◿) ● (2 x ⬛◻◿) ⬛◻◤● 6   73

● ◻ ◿ (5 x ⬛◻◿) 2 ●◤◣● 2 (5 x ⬛◻◿) ◣ ◻ ● 6   71

Amalie – *continued*

Knitting chart (worked from bottom, row 1, upward to row 69). Odd-numbered rounds are charted; all even rounds are knitted plain.

Charted round instructions (symbols read right to left)	end	round
● ◣ ◪ ◩ ◪ ◥ 2 ◪ ◤ (3 x ◥ ◪ ◤) ● ◭ ● (3 x ◥ ◪ ◤) ◥ ◪ 2 ◪ ◩ ◪ ◥ ●	6	69
● ◪ ◩ ◪ ● ◭ ● ◪ (2 x ◥ ◪ ◤) 2 ● ◭ ● 2 (2 x ◥ ◪ ◤) ◪ ● ◩ ◭ ● ◥ ◪ ◩ ●	6	67
● 5 ● 2 ◥ ◩ ◤ ● 2 (2 x ◥ ◪ ◤) ● ◭ ● (2 x ◥ ◪ ◤) 2 ● ◥ ◩ ● 2 ● 5 ●	6	65
● 3 ● 4 ◥ ◩ ◤ ● 3 ◥ ◪ ◤ 2 ● ◭ ● 2 ◥ ◪ ◤ 3 ● ◥ ◩ ● 4 ● 3 ●	6	63
● ◥ ● 5 ◥ ◩ ◤ ● (2 x ◥ ◪ ◤) ● ◆ ● (2 x ◥ ◪ ◤) ● ◥ ◩ ◤ 5 ● ◩ ●	6	61
● ◥ ● 5 ◥ ◩ ◤ 2 ● ◥ ◪ ◤ ● ◆ ● ◥ ◪ ◤ ● 2 ◥ ◩ ◤ 5 ● ◩ ●	6	59
● ◥ ● 5 ◥ ◩ ◤ 3 ● 4 ● ◆ ● 4 ● 3 ◥ ◩ ◤ 5 ● ◩ ●	6	57
● ◥ ● 5 ◥ ◩ ◤ 4 ● 2 ● ◆ ● 2 ● 4 ◥ ◩ ◤ 5 ● ◩ ●	6	55
● ◥ ● 12 ◪ ◆ ◪ 12 ● ◩ ●	6	53
● ◥ ● 10 ● ◆ ● 10 ● ◩ ●	6	51
● ◭ ● 8 ● ◆ ● 8 ● ◭ ●	6	49
● ◩ ◭ ● 6 ● ◆ ● 6 ● ◭ ◩ ●	6	47
● ◩ ◭ ◤ ● 4 ● ◆ ● 4 ● ◥ ◭ ◩ ●	6	45
● ◭ ◪ ◩ ◭ ● 2 ● ◆ ● 2 ● ◭ ◩ ◪ ◭ ●	6	43
● ◩ ◭ ◪ ◩ ● 3 ● ◭ ◩ ◪ ◭ ●	6	41
● ◭ ◪ ◩ ◪ ◭ ● ◩ ● ◭ ◪ ◩ ◪ ◭ ●	6	39
● ◩ ◭ ◪ ◩ ◤ 2 ● ◭ ● 2 ◥ ◪ ◭ ◩ ●	6	37
● ◭ ◪ ◩ ◪ ◭ ● ◩ ● ◭ ◪ ◩ ◪ ◭ ●	6	35
● ◩ ◭ ◪ ◩ ◤ 2 ● ◭ ● 2 ◥ ◪ ◭ ◩ ●	6	33
● (2 x ◥ ◪ ◤) ● ◭ ● (2 x ◥ ◪ ◤) ●	6	31
● ◥ ◪ ◤ ● ◩ ● ◥ ◪ ◤ ●	6	29
● 4 ● ◩ 3 ◥ ● 4 ●	6	27
● 2 ● ◩ 5 ◥ ● 2 ●	6	25
◪ ◤ 6 ● ◩ ◪ ●	6	23
◤ 6 ● ◩ ◥ ● 4 ●		21
◤ 6 ● ◩ 3 ◥ ● 2 ●		19
7 ● 7 ◪		17
6 ●		15
5 ●		13
4 ●		11
3 ●		9
2 ●		7
☐ ●		5
☐ ●		3
← ☐ →		1

Cast on 6 stitches
All rounds which are not mentioned are knitted plain

Margit

Knit with DMC Cébélia no. 20
Yarn requirement is about 15 gr
The stretched size is about 28 cm
1 Set double pointed needles 1.5 mm
1 cicular pin 1.5 mm at 40 cm
1 crochet hook 1.25 mm

Crochet edge: Crochet 4-4-4-4-5-5-5-4-4-4-4 stitches
with 7 chain stitches between

Cast on 8 stitches and knit 1 round plain
All rounds which are not mentioned are knitted plain

Lisette

Knit with DMC Cébélia no. 20
Yarn requirement is about 8 gr
The stretched size is about 21 cm
1 Set double pointed needles 1.5 mm
1 crochet hook 1.25 mm

Crochet edge: Crochet 5-6-6-4-5-4-6-6 stitches with 7 chain stitches between

← □ →	52
◢ (2 x 5 ●) (3 x 3 ●) 5 ● 5 ◣◢◢ ◣●	51
● 6 ● 4 ● 2 ●◆●● 2 ● 4 ● 6 ●◢ 3 ◣	49
● 5 ● (3 x 3 ●) 5 ●◢ 5 ◣	47
● 4 ● 2 ●◆●● 2 ● 4 ●◢ 7 ◣	45
● (3 x 3 ●) ◢ 9 ◣	43
● 2 ●◆●● 2 ●◢ 11 ◣	41
● 3 ●◢ 13 ◣	39
●◆● 7 ●◆●● 7	37
◢ 6 ●◆●● 6	35
◢◢◣ 5 ●◆●● 5	33
◢ 3 ◣ 4 ●◆●● 4	31
◢ 5 ◣ 3 ●◆●● 3	29
◢ 7 ◣ 2 ●◆●● 2	27
◢ 9 ◣ ●◆●● □	25
◢ 11 ◣◢●◆ ●	23
6 ●◆●● 7	21
5 ●◆●● 6	19
4 ●◆●● 5	17
3 ●◆●● 4	15
2 ●◆●● 3	13
□ ●◆●● 2	11
●◆●◆	9
●◣	7
●◆	5
← □ →	3
← □ →	1

Cast on 8 stitches
All rounds which are not mentioned are knitted plain

Christina

Knit with DMC Cébélia no. 30
Yarn requirement is about 5 gr
The stretched size is about 15 cm
1 Set double pointed needles 1.5 mm
1 crochet hook 1.25 mm

Crochet edge: Crochet 4-3-4-5-4-3-4-5 stitches with 9 chain stitches between

Cast on 12 stitches and knit 1 round plain
All rounds which are not mentioned are knitted plain

Thora

Knit with DMC Cébélia no. 20
Yarn requirement is about 8 gr
The stretched size is about 22 cm
1 Set double pointed needles 1.5 mm
1 cicular pin 1.5 mm at 40 cm
1 crochet hook 1.25 mm

Crochet edge: Crochet 4-3-3-3-4-4-3-2-3-2-3-4 stitches with 7 chain stitches between

Knitting chart (read from bottom to top, row numbers on the right):

Row	Embedded counts / notes
39	● 3 ... 3 ... 2 ... 3 ... 2
37	... 3 ... 4 ... 3 ... 3 ... 4
35	... 3 ... 3 ... 6 ... 6
33	... 8 ... 8
31	10 ... 3 ... 10
29	4 ● ... 5 ... 5 ... 4
27	3 ... 3 ... 4 ... 4 ... 3
25	5 ... 2 ... 3 ... 3 ... 2
23	7 ... (2 x ▢●) 2 ... 2 (2 x ●)
21	9 ... (7 x ●) ●
19	11 ... (3 x ●) ●
17	13
15	15
13	17
11	7 (3 x ●) ● 7
9	5 (3 x ●) ● 5
7	3 (3 x ●) ● 3
5	▢ (4 x ●)
3	▢ (2 x ●)
1	▢ ● ▢

Cast on 12 stitches and knit 1 round plain
All rounds which are not mentioned are knitted plain

Gurli

Repeat round 3 to 10 28 times. This is the center part

A

□◣● 3 (3 x ●▲● 3) ●◿	17
2 ◣●◆● (3 x ◿ ◣●◆●) ◿ 2	15
(4 x 3 ●▲●) 3	13
2 ● (3 x ◿ ◣●◆●) ◿ ◣● 2	11
□◣● (3 x 3 ●▲●) 3 ●◿	9
2 (4 x ◣●◆●◿) □	7
(4 x 3 ●▲●) 3	5
2 ● (3 x ◿ ◣●◆●) □ ◣● 2	3
‹ □ ›	1

Cast on 27 stitches and purl 1 round. Purl all even rounds
Crochet edge: Crochet (6 x 3 stitches with 7 chain stitches between) 3 stitches - 1 double crochet
- 3 stitches - 1 double crochet

D long side

●◣● (11 x ◿ ◣●◆●◿ ◣●◆●◿ ◣●◆●◿ ◣●◣●)	17
◿◣ (11 x ● 3 ●◆● 3 ●◆● 3 ●◆● 3 ●◿◣)	15
◿ 2 ◣ (11 x ●◆●▲●◆●◆●◆●▲●◆●◿ 2 ◣)	13
◿ 4 ◣ (11 x ●◿ ◣●◆●◿ ◣●◿ 4 ◣)	11
◿ 6 ◣ (11 x ● 3 ●◆● 3 ●◿ 6 ◣)	9
◿ 8 ◣ (11 x ●◆●◆●◆●◿ 8 ◣)	7
12 (11 x ●▲● 12)	5

C short side

●◣● (3 x ◿ ◣●◆●) ◿ ◣ ●◣●	17
◿◣● (3 x 3 ●◆●) 3 ●◿◣	15
◿ 2 ◣●◆●◿ (3 x ●◆) ●◿●◆●◆●◿ 2 ◣	13
◿ 4 ◣●◿ ◣●◆●◿ 4 ◣	11
◿ 6 ◣● 3 ●◆● 3 ●◿ 6 ◣	9
◿ 8 ◣ (3 x ●◆) ●◿ 8 ◣	7
2 ●▲● 12	5

Knit with DMC Cébélia no. 30
Yarn requirement is about 20 gr
The stretched size is about 16 x 59 cm
1 Set double pointed needles 1.5 mm
1 cicular pin 1.5 mm at 40 and 60 cm
1 crochet hook 1.25 mm

B corner

(7 x ◿ ◣●◆●) ◿◣	17
● (7 x 3 ●◆●) 3 ●	15
●◆●▲ (3 x ●◆) ●◿▲ (3 x ●◆) ●◿▲ (3 x ●◆) ●◿▲●◆●	13
● (3 x ◿ ◣●◆●) ◿ ◣●◣●	11
● (3 x 3 ●◆●) 3 ●	9
(7 x ●◆) ●	7
(3 x ●◆) ●	5

After round 4 the rounds are knitted in this order: B - C - B - D - B - C - B - D

12 ●◆●	3
←●◣►	1

Use 27 stitches from the short side, pick up 155 stitches from one
of the long sides, 27 stitches from the second short side and 155
stitches from the last long side.
Knit round 1-4.
All rounds which are not mentioned are knitted plain

Jenna

Crochet edge: Crochet 5-2-2-(19 x 3)-2-2 stitches with 7 chain stitches between

(knitting chart with rounds numbered on the right side)

3	81
7	79
11	77→8M
6	75
6	73
6	71
6 (2 x)	69
6 (3 x)	67
(4 x)	65 *
35 (5 x)	63
31 (6 x)	61
9 (7 x)	59 * * *
14 (8 x)	57
10 (9 x)	55
6 (4 x) (4 x)	53
2 (3 x) 2 2 (3 x)	51
(4 x) w (4 x)	49 * *
(4 x) (4 x)	47
(3 x) U (3 x)	45
(4 x) - - (4 x)	43 *
(4 x) (6 x) (4 x)	41
(3 x) (6 x -) (3 x)	39
(3 x) (6 x -) (3 x)	37
(2 x) (6 x -) (2 x)	35
(6 x -)	33
- - U U - -	31
U - - U U - - U	29
U U U U	27
U U 3	25
5	23
7	21
9	19
11	17
5 5	15
6 6	13
5 5	11
4 4	9
3 3	7
2 2	5
	3
	1

* in round 44 and 66 = knit 3 stitches in the 3 yarn over
*** in round 60 = knit 9 stitches in the 3 yarn over
** = w = clustering tic stitch

Cast on 6 stitches and knit 1 round plain
All rounds which are not mentioned are knitted plain

Clustering Tie Stitch

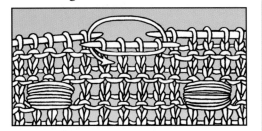

Knit 4 plain stitches on to a short extra needle. Wind the yarn round them 20 times. Place the stitches back on the right hand needle and continue. Knit them individually on the next row.

Knit with DMC Cébélia no. 20
Yarn requirement is about 25 gr
The stretched size is about 34 cm
1 Set double pointed needles 1.5 mm
1 cicular pin 1.5 mm at 40 and 60 cm
1 crochet hook 1.25 mm

Nanna

Knit with DMC Cébélia no. 30
Yarn requirement is about 4 gr
The stretched size is about 14 cm
1 Set double pointed needles 1.5 mm
1 crochet hook 1.25 mm

Crochet edge: Crochet 2-3-5-5-5-5-5-3-2-3 stitches with 7 chain stitches between

Cast on 8 stitches and knit 1 round plain
All rounds which are not mentioned are knitted plain

Hennie

Knit with DMC Cébélia no. 30
Yarn requirement is about 130 gr
The stretched size is about 150 cm
1 Set double pointed needles 1.5 mm
1 cicular pin 1.5 mm at 40, 60 and 100 cm
1 crochet hook 1.25 mm

Crochet edge: Crochet 3-3-3-3-3-4-4-4-4-3-4-4-4-4-4-3-3-3-3-3-3-3 stitches with 7 chain stitches between

- to be continued

Hennie – *continued*

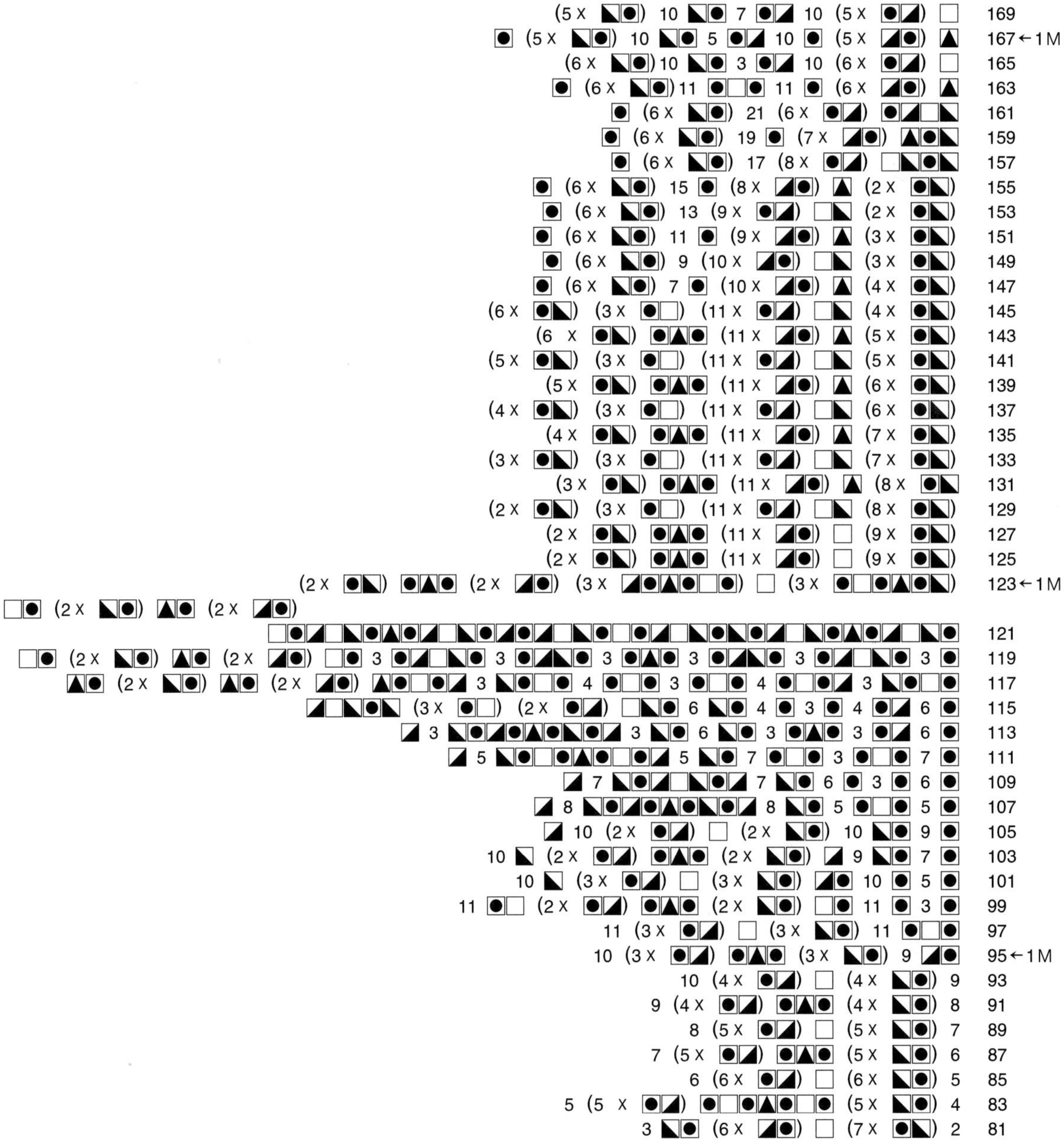

Row instruction (symbols)	Row #
(5 x ◣●) 10 ◣● 7 ●◢ 10 (5 x ●◢) □	169
● (5 x ◣●) 10 ◣● 5 ●◢ 10 ● (5 x ◢●) ▲	167 ←1 M
(6 x ◣●) 10 ◣● 3 ●◢ 10 (6 x ●◢) □	165
● (6 x ◣●) 11 ● □ ● 11 ● (6 x ◢●) ▲	163
● (6 x ◣●) 21 (6 x ●◢) ●◢ ◣	161
● (6 x ◣●) 19 ● (7 x ◢●) ▲●◢	159
● (6 x ◣●) 17 (8 x ●◢) □◣●◢	157
● (6 x ◣●) 15 ● (8 x ◢●) ▲ (2 x ●◣)	155
● (6 x ◣●) 13 (9 x ●◢) □◣ (2 x ●◣)	153
● (6 x ◣●) 11 ● (9 x ◢●) ▲ (3 x ●◣)	151
● (6 x ◣●) 9 (10 x ●◢) □◣ (3 x ●◣)	149
● (6 x ◣●) 7 ● (10 x ◢●) ▲ (4 x ●◣)	147
(6 x ●◣) (3 x ● □) (11 x ●◢) □◣ (4 x ●◣)	145
(6 x ●◣) ●◢▲● (11 x ◢●) ▲ (5 x ●◣)	143
(5 x ●◣) (3 x ● □) (11 x ●◢) □◣ (5 x ●◣)	141
(5 x ●◣) ●◢▲● (11 x ◢●) ▲ (6 x ●◣)	139
(4 x ●◣) (3 x ● □) (11 x ●◢) □◣ (6 x ●◣)	137
(4 x ●◣) ●◢▲● (11 x ◢●) ▲ (7 x ●◣)	135
(3 x ●◣) (3 x ● □) (11 x ●◢) □◣ (7 x ●◣)	133
(3 x ●◣) ●◢▲● (11 x ◢●) ▲ (8 x ●◣)	131
(2 x ●◣) (3 x ● □) (11 x ●◢) □◣ (8 x ●◣)	129
(2 x ●◣) ●◢▲● (11 x ◢●) □ (9 x ●◣)	127
(2 x ●◣) ●◢▲● (11 x ◢●) □ (9 x ●◣)	125
(2 x ●◣) ●◢▲● (2 x ◢●) (3 x ◢●▲● ●◢) □ (3 x ●◢ ●◢▲●◣)	123 ←1 M
□● (2 x ◣●) ▲● (2 x ◢●)	
◣●◢ ◣●◢▲●◢ ◣●◢◢ ◣●◢◢ ◣● ●◢ ◣●◢ ◣●◢◢ ◣●◢▲●◢ ◣●	121
□● (2 x ◣●) ▲● (2 x ◢●) □● 3 ◢● ●◢ 3 ◣●▲● 3 ●◢▲● 3 ◢●◣● 3 ●◢ ●◢ 3 ●	119
▲● (2 x ◣●) ▲● (2 x ◢●) ▲●◢ ●◢ 3 ◣● 4 ● ●◢ 3 ● 4 ● ●◢ 3 ◣● 3 ●	117
◢ ◣●◣ (3 x ● □) (2 x ●◢) □◣● 6 ◣● 4 ● 3 ● 4 ●◢ 6 ●	115
◢ 3 ◣●◢▲●◢▲●◢ 3 ◣● 6 ◣● 3 ●◢▲● 3 ●◢ 6 ●	113
◢ 5 ◣● ●◣●◢ 5 ◣● 7 ● 3 ● 7 ●	111
◢ 7 ◣●◢ ◣●◢ 7 ◣● 6 ● 3 ● 6 ●	109
◢ 8 ◣●◢▲●◢▲●◢ 8 ◣● 5 ● ● 5 ●	107
◢ 10 (2 x ●◢) □ (2 x ◣●) 10 ◣● 9 ●	105
10 ◣ (2 x ●◢) ●◢▲● (2 x ◣●) ◢ 9 ◣● 7 ●	103
10 ◣ (3 x ●◢) □ (3 x ◣●) ◢● 10 ● 5 ●	101
11 ●□ (2 x ●◢) ●◢▲● (2 x ◣●) □● 11 ● 3 ●	99
11 (3 x ●◢) □ (3 x ◣●) 11 ●□●	97
10 (3 x ●◢) ●◢▲● (3 x ◣●) 9 ◢●	95 ←1 M
10 (4 x ●◢) □ (4 x ◣●) 9	93
9 (4 x ●◢) ●◢▲● (4 x ◣●) 8	91
8 (5 x ●◢) □ (5 x ◣●) 7	89
7 (5 x ●◢) ●◢▲● (5 x ◣●) 6	87
6 (6 x ●◢) □ (6 x ◣●) 5	85
5 (5 x ●◢) ● □ ●◢▲● □ (5 x ◣●) 4	83
3 ◣● (6 x ◢●) □ (7 x ●◣) 2	81

Hennie - *continued*

Round
79
77→1M
75←1M
73→1M
71→1M
69
67
65
63
61
59
57
55
53
51
49
47
46
45
43
41
39
37
35→1M
33→1M
31→1M
29→1M
27
25
23
21
19→1M
17
15→1M
13
11→1M
9→1M
7
5
3
1

Cast on 8 stitches and knit 1 round plain
All rounds which are not mentioned are knitted plain

Until round 77 repeat the pattern 8 times
From round 79 to round 209 repeat the pattern 16 times
From round 211 to round 245 repeat the pattern 32 times

Martine

Knit with DMC Cébélia no. 20
Yarn requirement is about 10 gr
The stretched size is about 19 cm
1 Set double pointed needles 1.5 mm
1 crochet hook 1.25 mm

Crochet edge: Crochet 3 stitches with 7 chain stitches between

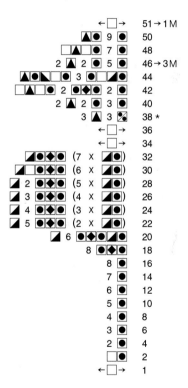

Cast on 8 stitches
All rounds which are not mentioned are knitted plain
* = in round 39: knit 3 stitches in the double yarn over (knit - purl - knit)

Ulla

Knit with DMC Cébélia no. 30
Yarn requirement is about 5 gr
The stretched size is about 17 cm
1 Set double pointed needles 1.5 mm
1 crochet hook 1.25 mm

Crochet edge: Crochet 3 stitches with 7 chain stitches between

```
                                    ←□→   45→1M
                      6 ● 11 ● 5           44
                 □ ◢ 4 ● 9 ● 4 ◣           42
              ◆ ● ◢ 4 ● 7 ● 4 ◣ ●          40
              ▲ ● ◢ 4 ● 5 ● 4 ◣ ●          38
          □ ▲ □ ● ◢ 4 ● 3 ● 4 ◣ ●          36
          2 ▲ 2 ● 5 ● □ ● 5 ●              34
            □ ◢ ● ▲ ● ◣ □ 9 ●              32
          □ ◢ ● ▲ ● ◣ ◣ □ 7 ●              30
        □ ◢ ● ▲ (3 x ● ◣) □ ● 5 ●          28
        □ ◢ ● ▲ (4 x ● ◣) □ ● 3 ●          26
      □ ◢ ● ▲ (5 x ● ◣) (2 x □ ●)          24
        □ ◢ ● ▲ (6 x ● ◣) □ ●              22
         (6 x ● ◣) ● ◆ ● 4                 20
         (5 x ● ◣) ● ◆ ● 4                 18
         (4 x ● ◣) ● ◆ ● 4                 16
         (3 x ● ◣) ● ◆ ● 4                 14
         (2 x ● ◣) ● ◆ ● 4                 12
             ● ◣ ● ◆ ● 4                   10
               ● ◆ ● 4                      8
                   ● 4                      6
                   ● 3                      4
                   ● 2                      2
                  ←□→                       1
```

Cast on 10 stitches and knit 1 round plain
All rounds which are not mentioned are knitted plain

Julie

Cast off loosly and stretch the finish work into an oval shape

Knit with DMC Cébélia no. 20
Yarn requirement is about 20 gr
The stretched size is about 30 x 40 cm
1 Set double pointed needles 1.5 mm
1 cicular pin 1.5 mm at 40 and 60 cm

Cast on 8 stitches and knit 1 round plain
All rounds which are not mentioned are knitted plain

Yrsa

Knit with DMC Cébélia no. 30
Yarn requirement is about 17 gr
The stretched size is about 28 x 28 cm
1 Set double pointed needles 1.5 mm
1 cicular pin 1.5 mm at 40 and 50 cm

Cast off loosly

←☐→ 77
☐● 76
●▲● 13 75→1M
◤◣ 5 ●◆● 5 ◤◣ 5 ●◆● 5 ◤◣ 73
▲●◣ 4 ●◆● 4 ◤●▲◣ 4 ●◆● 4 ◤●▲ 71→1M
◤◣●◣ 3 ●◆● 3 ◤●◤◣ ◤◣●◣ 3 ●◆● 3 ◤●◤◣ 69
▲ (2 x ●◣) 2 ●◆● 2 (2 x ◤●) ▲ (2 x ●◣) 2 ●◆● 2 (2 x ◤●) 67→1M
☐ (3 x ◣●) 3 (3 x ●◤) ☐ (3 x ◣●) 3 (3 x ●◤) 65
◆ (3 x ●◣) ●☐● (3 x ◤●) ◆ (3 x ●◣) ●☐● (3 x ◤●) 63
▲ (2 x ●◣) ● 3 ● (2 x ◤●) ▲ (2 x ●◣) ● 3 ● (2 x ◤●) 61→1M
☐ (3 x ◣●) ☐ (3 x ●◤) ☐ (3 x ◣●) ☐ (3 x ●◤) 59
▲ (2 x ●◣) ● 3 ● (2 x ◤●) ▲ (2 x ●◣) ● 3 ● (2 x ◤●) 57→1M
☐ (3 x ◣●) ☐ (3 x ●◤) ☐ (3 x ◣●) ☐ (3 x ●◤) 55
▲ (2 x ●◣) ● 3 ● (2 x ◤●) ▲ (2 x ●◣) ● 3 ● (2 x ◤●) 53→1M
☐ (3 x ◣●) ☐ (3 x ●◤) ☐ (3 x ◣●) ☐ (3 x ●◤) 51
◆ (2 x ●◣) ● 3 ● (2 x ◤●) ◆ (2 x ●◣) ● 3 ● (2 x ◤●) 49
◆●◣●☐ ●◤●◤● (3 x ▲●◣●◣●☐ ●◤●◤●) 47
◆●◣● 3 ●◤● (3 x ◤ ◣●◣● 3 ●◤●) 45
◆●◣●☐ ●◤● (3 x ◤ 3 ◣●◣●☐ ●◤●) 43
◆● 3 ● (3 x ◤ 5 ◣● 3 ●) 41
◆● ● ●◤ 3 ▲ 3 ◣● ●◤ 2 ●▲● 2 ◣● ●◤ 3 ▲ 3 ◣● ● 39
▲● 5 ●◆●● 5 ● (3 x ◤ ◣● ● 5 ●◆●● 5 ● 37
●▲● 4 ●◆● 4 ●◤ ◣● 3 ◤ ◣● 4 ●◆● 4 35
●▲● 3 ●◆● 3 ◤ ◣● 5 ◤ ◣● 3 ●◆● 3 33
●▲● 2 ●◆● 2 ◤ ◣● 2 ●▲● 2 ◤ ◣● 2 ●◆● 2 31
(2 x ●◆●☐) ●◤ ◣● 2 ●◤ ◣● 2 ◣● ◤● ●◆● 29
(2 x ●☐●) ●◤ ◣● 2 ●◤ 3 ◣● 2 ◣● ◤● (2 x ●☐) 27
☒◤● (2 x ◤ 2 ●) ◤ 5 ◣ (2 x ● 2 ◣) ●◤☒ 25
● 3 ● (2 x ◤ 2 ●) ▲ (2 x ● 2 ◣) ● 3 ● 23
●☐● (2 x ◤ 2 ●) ◤▲ (2 x ● 2 ◣)●☐● 21
● 3 ●◤ 2 ●◤ 3 ◣● 2 ◣● 3 ● 19
●☐ ●◤ 2 ●◤ 5 ◣● 2 ◣●☐● 17
● 3 ●◤ 7 ◣● 3 ● 15
●☐● ◤ 9 ◣●☐● 13
●☐ (11 x ◆) ●☐ 11
☐ Knit 11 stitches in the double yarn over ☐ 10
◣☒◤ 9
●▲◣●◣◤● 7
←☐→ 5
☒☒ 3
←☐→ 1

Cast on 8 stitches
All rounds which are not mentioned are knitted plain

Britta

Knit with DMC Cébélia no. 20
Yarn requirement is about 35 gr
The stretched size is about 35 x 45 cm
1 Set double pointed needles 1.5 mm
1 cicular pin 1.5 mm at 60 and 80 cm
1 crochet hook 1.25 mm

Center part A

```
5 ● 7 ●□ (14 x ◳) ●◣●□ 7 ●▲●□ 7 ● 5    55
5 ● 5 ● (14 x ◳) □●◣●□ 5 ● □▲□ ● 5 ● 5    53
5 ● 3 ●□ (14 x ◳) ●◣●□ 3 ● 2 ▲ 2 ● 3 ● 5    51
5 ●□ ● (14 x ◳) □●◣●□ ● 3 ▲ 3 ● □ ● 5    49
       5 ●□ (14 x ◳) □ ● □ ● 9 ● □ ● 5    47
5 ●□ (2 x ◳◳◳●▲●□) ◳◳◳●▲●□ 7 ● 5    45
5 ●□ (2 x ◳◳● □▲□ ● □) ◳◳● □▲□ ● 5 ● 5    43
5 ●□ (2 x ◳● 2 ▲ 2 ● □) ◳● 2 ▲ 2 ● 3 ● 5    41
5 ●□ ● 3 (2 x ▲ 3 ●▲● 3) ▲ 3 ● □ ● 5    39
          5 ● 9 (2 x ●◆● 9) ● 5    37
          5 ● 7 (2 x ●▲● 7) ● 5    35
          5 ● 5 (2 x ● □▲□ ● 5) ● 5    33
          5 ● 3 (2 x ● 2 ▲ 2 ● 3) ● 5    31
5 ●□ ● 3 ▲ 3 ●▲● 3 ▲ 3 ● □ ● 5    29
             5 ● 9 ●◆● 9 ● 5    27
             5 ● 7 ●▲● 7 ● 5    25
          5 ● 5 ● □▲□ ● 5 ● 5    23
          5 ● 3 ● 2 ▲ 2 ● 3 ● 5    21
          5 ●□ ● 3 ▲ 3 ● □ ● 5    19
                5 ● 9 ● 5    17
                5 ● 7 ● 5    15
                5 ● 5 ● 5    13
                5 ● 3 ● 5    11
                5 ●◆● 5     9
                4 ●◆● 4     7
                3 ●◆● 3     5
                2 ●◆● 2     3
                □●◆●□      1
```

Cast on 3 stitches, purl back

- to be continued

Britta – *continued*

Row numbers (right side of chart):

137, 135, 133, 131, 129, 127, 125, 123, 121, 119, 117, 115, 113, 111, 109, 107, 105, 103, 101, 99, 97, 95, 93, 91, 89, 87, 85, 83, 81, 79, 77, 75, 73, 71, 69, 67, 65, 63, 61, 59, 57

Britta – *continued*

Crochet edge: Crochet 4-4-4-3-4-4-4-7 stitches with 7 chain stitches between

Part C

Chart row	Row number
●●▲ (2 x ●◢) 2 ◥● 17 ●◢ 2 ◥	45
●◥●▲●◢●◢▲◥◿◢● 15 ●▲◥◿◢▲	43
●◥●▲●◢●◢ (2 x ◥◿◢) ▲● 13 ●▲ (2 x ◥◿◢) ▲	41
(3 x ●▲) ●◢ (3 x ◥◿◢) ◥● 11 ●◢ (3 x ◥◿◢) ◥	39
●◢▲ ▲ ●◥● (4 x ◥◿◢) ●●●● (4 x ◥◿◢)	37 *
◢● 2 ▲ 2 ●◥● □ (3 x ◥◿◢) □◿ (3 x ◥◿◢) □●	35
◢● 3 ▲ 3 ●◥● 2 (2 x ◥◿◢) 2 ◿ 2 (2 x ◥◿◢) 2 ●	33
◆● 9 ◆●◆ 3 ◥◿◢ 3 ◿ 3 ◥◿◢ 3 ●	31
▲● 7 ●▲● (2 x ◥◿◢) ◿ (2 x ◥◿◢) ●	29
◢ ◥● 5 ●◢ ◥● ◥◿◢ ◥◿◢ ●	27
◢ 3 ◥● 3 ●◢ 3 ◥● 4 ◿ 4 ●	25
◢ 5 ◥● ●◢ 5 ◥● 2 ◿ 2 ●	23
9 ● 9 ● 2 ●	21
18 ◿	19

* On the plain round knit 11 stitches in the 4 yarn over.

Part B

Chart	Row number
←□→	14-18
◥◿◢	13
◥◿◢	11
◥◿◢	9
◥◿◢	7
◥◿◢	5
←□→	1-4

Pick up 285 stitches for the edge, with the 3 stitches left on the needle it makes 288 stitches.
Knit on a circula needle following pattern B. After round 18 knit pattern C

Louise

Crochet edge: 7 x (3 stitches with 7 chain stitches between) 5 stitches with 7 chain stitches, 7 x (3 stitches with 7 chain stitches between) 3 x (3 stitches with a double crochet between). Finish with 7 chain stitches in the first chain.

← □ → 234 → 2M
● ▲ ●▲● (3 x ◣●) 35 (3 x ●◢) ●▲ 233
● ▲ ● ▲ (3 x ●◣) ● 33 (3 x ●◢) ● ▲ 231
●◀● 2 ▲ 2 (3 x ●◣) ● 11 ● (make 7 stitches in the next stitch) ● 11 ● (3 x ◢●) 2 ▲ 2 229
●◢ 2 ◣● 3 ▲ 3 (3 x ●◣) ● (11 x □●) (3 x ◢●) 3 ▲ 3 227
●◢ 2 ◣● 4 ▲ 4 (3 x ●◣) ● (5 x □●) (3 x ◢●) 4 ▲ 4 225
●◢ 2 ◣● 5 ▲ 5 (3 x ●◣) ● 3 ● (3 x ◢●) 5 ▲ 5 223
●◢◈◣● 13 (3 x ●◣) ● ● (3 x ◢●) 13 221
▲◢▲◣● 11 ◈◣●◣● 3 ●◢●◢◈ 11 ● 219
◢ 2 ◣◢ 2 ◣● 9 ◈◣●◣● ●◢●◢◈ 9 217
◢ 4 ◣◢ 4 ◣● 7 ◈◣● 3 ●◢◈ 7 ● 215
◢ 6 ◣◢ 6 ◣● 5 ◈◣● ●◢◈ 5 ● 213
◢ 8 ◣◢ 8 ◣● 3 ◈ 3 ◈ 3 ● 211
◢ 10 ◣◢ 10 ◣●◣●◈ ◈◢ 209
◢ 12 ◣◢ 12 ◣●●▽● 207
← – → 201- 205
◢ 9 ● 199
◢ 9 ● 197
◢ 9 ● 195
▲◈◢ 6 ● 193
◢ 9 ● 191
▲◈▲◣◈◢ 2 ● 189
◢ 9 ● 187
◢ 4 ◣◈◢ ● 185
◢ 9 ● 183
◢ 9 ● 181
◢ 9 ● 179
10 ● 177
← – → 171- 175
← □ → 170 → 10M

Knit with DMC Cébélia no. 30
Yarn requirement is about 110 gr
The stretched size is about 84 cm
1 Set double pointed needles 1.5 mm
1 cicular pin 1.5 mm at 40, 60, 80 and 100 cm
1 crochet hook 1.25 mm

- to be continued

Louise – *continued*

	Row
(6 x ●◣) ● 3 ◪◀◪◀◪◪ 3 ◪◀◪◪◀◪ 3 (6 x ●◢) ●◆	169
(6 x ●◣) ● 31 (6 x ●◢) ●◆	167
(6 x ●◣) ● 29 (6 x ●◢) ●◆	165
(6 x ●◣) ● 27 (6 x ●◢) ●▲	163
(6 x ●◣) ● 25 (7 x ●◢) ☐▲	161 ←1M
(7 x ◣●) 23 (7 x ●◢) 3	159 ←1M
2 (7 x ◣●) 21 (7 x ●◢) 3	157
●◀● (6 x ◣●) 19 (6 x ●◢) ●◀●◆	155
● 4 ▲ (6 x ●◣) ● 17 ● (6 x ◢●) ▲ 4 ●◆	153
● 5 (7 x ◣●) 15 (7 x ●◢) 5 ●▲	151 →1M
6 (6 x ●◣) ● 2 (make 9 stitches in the next stitch) 2 ● (6 x ◢●) 6 ●◢▲▲◣●	149
☐●◿●☐ ● (6 x ◣●) 3 (6 x ●◢) ● ☐●◿●☐ ● (3 x ▲◢)	147
◀ (6 x ●◣) ● ☐ ● (6 x ◢●) ◀●▲◣●▲●◣●	145
6 (5 x ●◣) ● 3 ● (5 x ◢●) 6 ●◢▲ ◣● ▲ ●◣●	143
6 (5 x ●◣) ●☐● (5 x ◢●) 6 ●◢ ▲ 2 ●▲● 2 ▲ ◣●	141
6 (4 x ●◣) ● 3 ● (4 x ◢●) 6 ●◢ 2 ▲ 3 ●▲● 3 ▲ 2 ◣●	139
☐●◿●☐ (4 x ●◣) ●☐● (4 x ◢●) ☐●◿●☐ ●◢ 3 ▲ 4 ●▲● 4 ▲ 3 ◣●	137
◀ (3 x ●◣) ● 3 ● (3 x ◢●) ◀● 11 ●▲● 11 ●	135
6 (3 x ●◣) ●▲● (3 x ◢●) 6 ● 9 ●▲▲▲● 9 ●	133
6 (3 x ●◣) ●▲ (3 x ●◢) ● 6 ● 7 ● ☐ ▲ ☐ ●▲● ☐ ▲ ☐ ● 7 ●	131
6 (3 x ●◣) ●☐ (3 x ●◢) ● 6 ● 5 ● 2 ▲ 2 ●▲● 2 ▲ 2 ● 5 ●	129
☐●◿●☐ ● (2 x ◣●) 3 (2 x ●◢) ● ☐●◿●☐ ● 3 ● 3 ▲ 3 ●▲● 3 ▲ 3 ● 3 ●	127
◀●◣●◣●▲●◢●◢●◀● ● 4 ▲ 4 ●▲● 4 ▲ 4 ●	125
6 ●◣●◣●▲●◢●◢● 6 ● 11 ●▲● 11 ●	123
6 ●◣● ☐ ●◢▲◢● 6 ● 9 ●▲▲▲● 9 ●	121
6 ●◣● 3 ●◢● 6 ● 7 ● ☐ ▲ ☐ ●▲● ☐ ▲ ☐ ● 7 ●	119
☐●◿●☐ ●◣●▲●◢● ☐●◿●☐ ● 5 ● 2 ▲ 2 ●▲● 2 ▲ 2 ● 5 ●	117
◀●◣●▲●◢● 3 ● 3 ▲ 3 ●▲● 3 ▲ 3 ● 3 ●	115
6 ●◣● ☐ ●◢● 6 ● ☐ ● 4 ▲ 4 ●▲● 4 ▲ 4 ● ☐ ●	113
6 ● 3 ● 6 ● 11 ●▲● 11 ●	111
6 ●▲● 6 ● 9 ●▲▲▲● 9 ●	109
☐●◿●☐ ●▲● ☐●◿●☐ ● 7 ● ☐ ▲ ☐ ●▲● ☐ ▲ ☐ ● 7 ●	107
◀●▲●◀● 5 ● 2 ▲ 2 ●▲● 2 ▲ 2 ● 5 ●	105
6 ●▲● 6 ● 3 ● 3 ▲ 3 ●▲● 3 ▲ 3 ● 3 ●	103
6 ●▲● 6 ● ☐ ● 4 ▲ 4 ●▲● 4 ▲ 4 ● ☐ ●	101

70

	Row
6 ●▲● 6 ● 11 ●▲● 11 ●	99
□●▽● ●▲● ●▽● ● 9 ●▲▲▲● 9 ●	97
◀●▲●◀● 7 ● ▲ ●▲● ● 7 ●	95
6 ●▲● 6 ● 5 ● 2 ▲ 2 ●▲● 2 ▲ 2 ● 5 ●	93
6 ●▲● 6 ● 3 ● 3 ▲ 3 ●▲● 3 ▲ 3 ● 3 ●	91
6 ●▲● 6 ● ● 4 ▲ 4 ●▲● 4 ▲ 4 ● ●	89
□●▽● ●▲● ●▽● ● 11 ●▲● 11 ●	87
◀●▲●◀● 9 ●▲◀● 9 ●	85
6 ●▲● 6 ● 7 ●▲●▲●▲● 7 ●	83
6 ●▲● 6 ● 5 ● ▲ ●▲● ▲ ● 5 ●	81
6 ●▲● 6 ● 3 ● 2 ▲ 2 ●▲● 2 ▲ 2 ● 3 ●	79
□●▽● (3 x □●) ▽● ● ● 3 ▲ 3 ●▲● 3 ▲ 3 ● ●	77
◀●◀● 9 ●▲● 9 ●	75
12 ● 7 ●▲◀● 7 ●	73
12 ● 5 ●▲●▲●▲● 5 ●	71
12 ● 3 ● ▲ ●▲● ▲ ● 3 ●	69
3 (make 6 stiches in the next stitch) 3 ●□● 2 ▲ 2 ●▲● 2 ▲	
2 ●□● (make 12 stitches in the next stitch) ●□● 2 ▲ 2 ●▲● 2 ▲ 2 ● □ ●	67
□●▽● ● 7 ●◆● 7 ●▲● 7 ●◆● 7 ●	65
◀● 5 ●◆● 5 ●▲● 5 ●◆● 5 ●	63
6 ● 3 ●▲● 3 ●▲●▲●▲● 3 ●▲● 3 ●	61
6 (2 x ●□) ▲ (2 x □●) ▲●▲● ▲ (2 x ●□) ▲ (2 x □●)	59
6 ● 5 ● 2 ▲ 2 ●▲● 2 ▲ 2 ● 5 ●	57
□●▽● ● 3 ● 3 ▲ 3 ●▲● 3 ▲ 3 ● 3 ●	55
◀● ● 4 ▲ 4 ●▲● 4 ▲ 4 ● ●	53
6 ● 11 ●▲● 11 ●	51
6 ● 9 ●▲◀● 9 ●	49
6 ● 7 (3 x ●▲) ● 7 ●	47
□●▽● ● 5 ● ▲ ●▲● ▲ ● 5 ●	45
◀● 3 ● 2 ▲ 2 ●▲● 2 ▲ 2 ● 3 ●	43
6 ●□● 3 ▲ 3 ●▲● 3 ▲ 3 ● □ ●	41
6 ● 9 ●▲● 9 ●	39
6 ● 7 ●▲◀● 7 ●	37
□●▽● ● 5 (3 x ●▲) ● 5 ●	35
◀● 3 ● ▲ ●▲● ▲ ● 3 ●	33
6 ●□● 2 ▲ 2 ●▲● 2 ▲ 2 ● □ ●	31
6 ● 7 ●▲● 7 ●	29
6 ● 5 ●▲◀● 5 ●	27
□●▽● ● 3 (3 x ●▲) ● 3 ●	25
◀ (2 x ●□) ▲ ●▲● ▲ (2 x □●)	23
6 ● 5 ●◆● 5 ●	21
6 ● 3 ●▲● 3 ●	19
6 (2 x ●□) ▲ (2 x □●)	17
□●▽● ● 5 ●	15
◀● 3 ●	13
6 ● ●	11
6 ●	9
5 ◣	7
2 ●◆● 2	5
□●◆● □	3
□●	1

◀ = Slip 3 stitches, knit 3, pass slipped stitches over

Cast on 12 stitches and knit 2 rounds plain
All rounds which are not mentioned are knitted plain

Hansigne

Crochet edge: Crochet (8 x4) 5 (8 x 4) stitches with 7 chain stitches between, 1 double crochet, 3 stitches, 1 double crochet

```
←□→                                          110←1M
←□→                                          106-109
4 (6x ◣) 3 ● (4x 2 ●) (11x □●) (4x 2 ●) 3 (6x ◢) 3    105
←□→                                          100-104
▲● (6x ◣) 3 ● (4x 2 ●) (9x □●) (4x 2 ●) 3 (6x ◢) ●    99
● ●▲● 51 ●▲                                  97
▲● ● ● 51 ● ●                                95
◢ ◣●▲● (5x ◣) (2x 2 ●) (13x □●) 2 ● 2 (5x ◢) ●▲●    93
◢ 3 ◣● ● 41 ● ●                              91
● ●▲● ● ◣● ●▲● 37 ●▲●                        89
◢ ●●◢ (2x ◣●) ●◣◣◣ 4 ● (11x □●) 4 ◢◢◢● ●    87
◢● ◢ 3 ◣● ● ●▲● ●▲● 27 ● ●                   85
(2x ◢ ●) ▲● (2x ◣ ●) ●▲● 27 ●              83
(2x ◢ □ ●) ◢ (3x ◣●) ▲●◣◣ 2 ● (7x □●) 2 ◢◢▲●◢    81
(2x □●) ◢● (3x ◣●) ● 19 ● ●              79
◢ ●◢ (2x ●◢) □ (2x ◣●) ● ◣● 15 ●▲●        77
(2x ◢ □ ●) (2x ◢●) ◢ (2x ●◣) (2x ◣ ●) ● ●◣◣◣ 2 (3x ● □) ● 2 ◢◢▲● ●    75
◢ □●◢ (3x ●◢) □ (3x ◣●) (2x ◣●) ▲● 11 ●▲●    73
◢ ●◢ (4x ◣●) □ (4x ●◢) ● ● ◣● ● ● (2x 4 ●□ ●)    71
◢ 2 ●□ (3x ◣●) 3 (3x ●◢) □ ● 2 ◣●▲● 5 ●▲●    69
◢ ◣●▲● ● (3x ◣●) □ (3x ●◢) ●▲● ◣● ● 5 ● ●    67
2 ●◢ (2x ◣●) ◣● 3 ●◢ (2x ●◢) ◣● 2 ●▲● ●▲●    65
◢ ◣● 2 ◣●□ (2x ◣●) □ (2x ●◢) ●◢ 2 ●◢ ◣● (3x □●)    63
5 ● 2 ◣● ◣● 3 ●◢ ●◢ 2 ● 5 ●▲●                61
3 ●▲● 2 ◣● ◣● (2x □ ●◢) 2 ●▲● 3 ● ●          59
2 ●◢ ◣● 2 ◣● 5 ●◢ 2 ●◢ ◣● 2 ●                57→1M
3 ◣ (2x ● 2 ◣) ● 3 ● (2x ◢ 2 ●) ◢          55
5 (2x ● 2 ◣) ●□● (2x ◢ 2 ●) 3              53
4 ◣● 2 ◣● 7 (2x ●◢ 2)                      51
6 ● 2 ◣● 5 ●◢ 2 ● 4                        49
4 ●▲● 2 ◣● 3 ●◢ 2 ●▲● 2                    47
3 ●◢ ◣● ◣● 2 ◣● ●◢ 2 ●◢ ◣●                 45
3 ◣● 2 ◣● 7 ●◢ 2 ●◢                        43
5 ● 2 ◣● 5 ●◢ 2 ● 3                        41
4 ◣● 2 ◣● 3 (2x ●◢ 2)                      39
6 ● 2 ◣● ●◢ 2 ● 4                          37
5 ◣● 7 ●◢ 3                               35
7 (2x ● 5)                                33
6 ◣● 3 ●◢ 4                               31
8 ● □ ● 6                                 29
8 ● 6                                     27
←□→                                       25
☒ 5                                       23
▲● 3 ●                                    22
3 ●▲●                                     20
●◆● 3                                     18
(2x □●) ▲● □●                             16
▲● 3 ●                                    14
3 ● □●                                    12
● ● ●▲                                    10
▲● ● ●                                    8
3 ●                                       6
2 ●                                       4
□ ●                                       2
```

Knit with DMC Cébélia no. 20
Yarn requirement is about 35 gr
The stretched size is about 45 cm
1 Set double pointed needles 1.5 mm
1 cicular pin 1.5 mm at 60 cm
1 crochet hook 1.25 mm

Cast on 8 stitches and knit 1 round plain
All rounds which are not mentioned are knitted plain

Dorthe

Crochet edge: Crochet 5-4-4-4-3-4-4-4-5-5 stitches with
7 chain stitches

```
                                    ←□→        98←1M
        2     2 (2× ●)   % 23 %    □        97
        4     4 (2× ●)   % 19 % (2× )        95
        6     6 (2× ●)   % 15 % (2× )        93
        8     8 (2× ●)   % 11 % (2× )        91
        10    10 (2× ●)   % 7 % (2× )        89
        12    12  ●  ● % % ●        87
           14    14  ● 2 ● 3 ● 3 ●        85
        5 ● 11    11 ● 5 ● 2 %  2 ●        83
      ● 3 ● 12    12 ● 3 ● 2  2        81
      ● □ ● 13    13 □ ● 2  2        79
    ● 5 ● ● 6    6 ● ● 5 ● 2  2        77
  ● 3 ● □ ● 6    6 ● □ ● 3 ● 2  2        75
  ● □ ● 2   2 ● 13 ● 2  2 ● □ ● 2  2        73
        ● 7 ● 11 ● 7 ● %  2        71
      ● 5 ● ● 7 ● ● 5 ● 3 % 3        69
    ● 3 ● □ ● 5 ● □ ● 3 ● 4 % 4        67
  ● □ ● 2   2 ● 3 ● 2   2 ● ● 2  2        65
      ● 7 ● ● ● 7 ● 2  2        63
    ● 5 ● ● ● 5 ● 2 (2× % ) 2        61
    ● 3 ● ● ● 3 ● 2 (3× % ) 2        59
  □ ● ● ● □ ● 3 (4× % ) 3        57
    □ ● ● 2 (5× % ) 2        55
      4 %  (4× % ) %  3        53
        3 (5× % ) 2        51
      4 %  (4× % ) %  3        49
        3 (5× % ) 2        47
      4 %  (4× % ) %  3        45
    ● 3 % (3× % ) % 3 ●        43
    ● 3 % (2× % ) % 3 ●        41
     ● 3 (2× %  ) % 3 ●        39
    □  ● 2 (2× % ) 2 ●        37
    2  2 ● 3 % 4        35
        3  3 ● 7 ●        33
        4  4 ● 5 ●        31
        5  5 ● 3 ●        29
        6  6 ● □ ●        27
        7  7 ●        25→1M
        7  7 %        23→1M
        7  7 %        21→1M
        15 %        19→1M
        13 %        17→1M
        11 %        15→1M
        9 %        13→1M
        7 %        11→1M
        5 %        9→1M
        3 %        7→1M
        □ %        5
        ←□→        3
        ←□→        1
```

Knit with DMC Cébélia no. 20
Yarn requirement is about 30 gr
The stretched size is about 41 cm
1 Set double pointed needles 1.5 mm
1 cicular pin 1.5 mm at 40 and 60 cm
1 crochet hook 1.25 mm

Cast on 10 stitches
All rounds which are not mentioned are knitted plain

Conny

Knit with DMC Cébélia no. 20
Yarn requirement is about 11 gr
The stretched size is about 25 cm
1 Set double pointed needles 1.5 mm
1 cicular pin 1.5 mm at 40 cm
1 crochet hook 1.25 mm

Crochet edge: Crochet 3-2-3-2 stitches with 9 chain stitches between,
3-3 stitches with 1 chain stitch between

```
                                        ←□→    56
          ◤ ◣●◔●◣● 3 ●◤●◤◢    55
          ◤ 3 ◣●◔●◔●◔◆●◤●◤◢    53
                ◤ 5 ◣●◣● 3 ●◤◢    51
                ◤ 7 ◣●◔●◆●◤◢    49
                      ◤ 9 ◣● 3 ●    47
      (2 x ◤ 11 ◣●◆●) ◤ 11 ◣●◣◢◢    45
      (2 x 6 ●◆● 6 ◢) 6 ●◆● 6 ●   ● 43
        (2 x 5 ●◆● 5 ◤ ◣) 5 ●◆● 6    41
        (2 x 4 ●◆● 4 ◤ 3 ◣) 4 ●◆● 5    39
        (2 x 3 ●◆● 3 ◤ 5 ◣) 3 ●◆● 4    37
        (2 x 2 ●◆● 2 ◤ 7 ◣) 2 ●◆● 3    35
        (2 x □ ●◆● ◤ 9 ◣) □ ●◆● 2    33
          (2 x ●◆●◤ 11 ◣) ●◆●□    31
      ● 6 ●◆● 6 ◢ 6 ●◆● 6 ●□    29
          5 ●◆● 5 ◤ ◣ 5 ●◆● 6    27
        4 ●◆● 4 ◤ 3 ◣ 4 ●◆● 5    25
        3 ●◆● 3 ◤ 5 ◣ 3 ●◆● 4    23
        2 ●◆● 2 ◤ 7 ◣ 2 ●◆● 3    21
          □ ●◆● ◤ 9 ◣ □ ●◆● 2    19
            ●◆●◤ 11 ◣●◆●□    17
          ● 6 ●◆● 6 ●□    15
                5 ●◆● 6    13
                4 ●◆● 5    11
                3 ●◆● 4    9
                2 ●◆● 3    7
                □ ●◆● 2    5
                      ●◆    3
                      ←□→    1
```

Cast on 8 stitches
All rounds which are not mentioned are knitted plain

77

Alma

Knit with DMC Cébélia no.
Yarn requirement is about 105 gr
The stretched size is about 75 cm
1 Set double pointed needles 1.5 mm
1 cicular pin 1.5 mm at 40, 60, 80 and 100 cm
1 crochet hook 1.25 mm

Finish off or make a round of picots

←☐→	180 → 2 M
● 7 ●▲	179
● 5 ●◢▲	177
● 3 ●◢ 3 ◣	175 → 3 M
●◣●☐ ●◢◢▲☐ ◣	173
● 3 ●◢ 3 ◣	171
● ☐●◢ 5 ◣	169
▲ 19	167 → 1 M
▲ 21	165 → 1 M
▲ 23	163 → 1 M
▲ 25	161 → 1 M
▲● (13 x ☐●)	159 → 1 M
▲ 15	157 → 1 M
▲ 17	155 → 1 M
▲ 19	153 → 1 M
▲ 21	151 → 1 M
▲● (11 x ☐●)	149 → 1 M
▲ 13	147 → 1 M
▲ 15	145 → 1 M
▲ 17	143 → 1 M
▲● (9 x ☐●)	141 → 1 M
▲ 11	139 → 1 M
▲ 13	137 → 1 M
▲● (7 x ☐●)	135 → 2 M
● 7 ●▲	133
● 5 ●◢▲	131
● 3 ●◢◢●▲◣▲	129 → 1 M
☐ ●◣●◢▲ ◣●◢◢●	127 → 1 M
●◣●● 3 ●◢◢▲	125
●◣●☐ ●◢◢▲◢ ◣	123
● 3 ●◢ 3 ◣	121

Make it just the size you want by repeating from
round 71 to 119

- to be continued

Chart	Row
● ● ◢ 5 ◣	119
▲ 19	117→1 M
▲ 21	115→1 M
▲ 23	113→1 M
▲ 25	111→1 M
▲● (13 x □●)	109→1 M
▲ 15	107→1 M
▲ 17	105→1 M
▲ 19	103→1 M
▲ 21	101→1 M
▲● (11 x □●)	99→1 M
▲ 13	97→1 M
▲ 15	95→1 M
▲ 17	93→1 M
▲● (9 x □●)	91→1 M
▲ 11	89→1 M
▲ 13	87→1 M
▲● (7 x □●)	85→2 M
● 7 ●▲	83
● 5 ●◢ ◣	81
● 3 ●◢●▲●◣	79→1 M
□●◣●◢ ◣●◢●	77→1 M
●◣●● 3 ●◢●▲	75
●◣●●● ●◢●◢ ◣	73
● 3 ●◢ 3 ◣	71
● ● ◢ 5 ◣	69
▲ 19	67→1 M
▲ 21	65→1 M
▲ 23	63→1 M
▲ 25	61→1 M
▲● (13 x □●)	59→1 M
▲ 15	57→1 M
▲ 17	55→1 M
▲ 19	53→1 M
▲ 21	51→1 M
▲● (11 x □●)	49→1 M
▲ 13	47→1 M
▲ 15	45→1 M
▲ 17	43→1 M
▲● (9 x □●)	41→1 M
▲ 11	39→1 M
▲ 13	37→1 M
▲● (7 x □●)	35→2 M
● 7 ●▲	33
● 5 ●◢ ◣	31
● 3 ●◢●▲●◣	29→1 M
□●◣●◢ ◣●◢●	27→1 M
●◣●● 3 ●◢●▲	25
●◣●●● ●◢●◢ ◣	23
● 3 ●◢ 3 ◣	21
● ● ● 7	19
□●	13
□●	8
□●	4
□●	1

Cast on 6 stitches
All rounds which are not mentioned are knitted plain

Picot

Make 3-4 or 5 chain stitches depending on how larger you want the picot to be. Make a ring of chain stitches by doing a slip stitch in the first chain stitch.